Singapore MATH PRACTICE

LEVEL 2B

Appropriate for Students in GRADE 3

Thinking Kids®
An imprint of Carson-Dellosa Publishing LLC
Greensboro, North Carolina

W9-CFL-153

Visit *carsondellosa.com* for correlations to Common Core, state, national, and Canadian provincial standards.

Copyright © 2009 Singapore Asia Publishers PTE LTD.

Thinking Kids®
An imprint of Carson-Dellosa Publishing LLC
PO Box 35665
Greensboro, NC 27425 USA

ISBN 978-0-7682-4002-3
07-224197784

INTRODUCTION TO SINGAPORE MATH

Welcome to Singapore Math! The math curriculum in Singapore has been recognized worldwide for its excellence in producing students highly skilled in mathematics. Students in Singapore have ranked at the top in the world in mathematics on the *Trends in International Mathematics and Science Study* (TIMSS) in 1993, 1995, 2003, and 2008. Because of this, Singapore Math has gained in interest and popularity in the United States.

Singapore Math curriculum aims to help students develop the necessary math concepts and process skills for everyday life and to provide students with the ability to formulate, apply, and solve problems. Mathematics in the Singapore Primary (Elementary) Curriculum cover fewer topics but in greater depth. Key math concepts are introduced and built-on to reinforce various mathematical ideas and thinking. Students in Singapore are typically one grade level ahead of students in the United States.

The following pages provide examples of the various math problem types and skill sets taught in Singapore.

At an elementary level, some simple mathematical skills can help students understand mathematical principles. These skills are the counting-on, counting-back, and crossing-out methods. Note that these methods are most useful when the numbers are small

1. The Counting-On Method

Used for addition of two numbers. Count on in 1s with the help of a picture or number line.

$$7 + 4 = \mathbf{11}$$

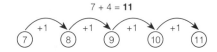

2. The Counting-Back Method

Used for subtraction of two numbers. Count back in 1s with the help of a picture or number line.

$$16 - 3 = \mathbf{13}$$

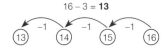

3. The Crossing-Out Method

Used for subtraction of two numbers. Cross out the number of items to be taken away. Count the remaining ones to find the answer.

$$20 - 12 = \mathbf{8}$$

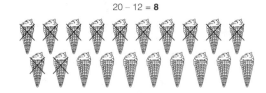

A **number bond** shows the relationship in a simple addition or subtraction problem. The number bond is based on the concept "part-part-whole." This concept is useful in teaching simple addition and subtraction to young children.

To find a whole, students must add the two parts.
To find a part, students must subtract the other part from the whole.

The different types of number bonds are illustrated below.

1. Number Bond (single digits)

3 (part) + 6 (part) = **9** (whole)
9 (whole) – 3 (part) = **6** (part)
9 (whole) – 6 (part) = **3** (part)

2. Addition Number Bond (single digits)

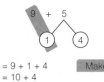

$$= 9 + 1 + 4$$
$$= 10 + 4$$
$$= \mathbf{14}$$

Make a ten first.

3. Addition Number Bond (double and single digits)

$$= 2 + 5 + 10$$
$$= 7 + 10$$
$$= \mathbf{17}$$

Regroup 15 into 5 and 10.

4. Subtraction Number Bond (double and single digits)

$$10 - 7 = 3$$
$$3 + 2 = \mathbf{5}$$

5. Subtraction Number Bond (double digits)

$$10 - 5 = 5$$
$$10 - 10 = 0$$
$$5 + 0 = \mathbf{5}$$

Students should understand that multiplication is repeated addition and that division is the grouping of all items into equal sets.

1. Repeated Addition (Multiplication)

Mackenzie eats 2 rolls a day. How many rolls does she eat in 5 days?

$$2 + 2 + 2 + 2 + 2 = 10$$
$$5 \times 2 = 10$$

She eats **10** rolls in 5 days.

2. The Grouping Method (Division)

Mrs. Lee makes 14 sandwiches. She gives all the sandwiches equally to 7 friends. How many sandwiches does each friend receive?

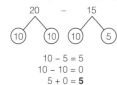

$$14 \div 7 = 2$$

Each friend receives **2** sandwiches.

One of the basic but essential math skills students should acquire is to perform the 4 operations of whole numbers and fractions. Each of these methods is illustrated below.

1. The Adding-Without-Regrouping Method

```
  H  T  O
  3  2  1
+ 5  6  8
─────────
  8  8  9
```
O: Ones
T: Tens
H: Hundreds

Since no regrouping is required, add the digits in each place value accordingly.

2. The Adding-by-Regrouping Method

```
   H  T  O
  ¹4  9  2
+  1  5  3
──────────
   6  4  5
```
O: Ones
T: Tens
H: Hundreds

In this example, regroup 14 tens into 1 hundred 4 tens.

Singapore Math Practice Level 2B

3. The Adding-by-Regrouping-Twice Method

```
  H T O
 ¹2 ¹8 6          O: Ones
+  3 6 5          T: Tens
-----------       H: Hundreds
   6 5 1
```

Regroup twice in this example.
First, regroup 11 ones into 1 ten 1 one.
Second, regroup 15 tens into 1 hundred 5 tens.

4. The Subtracting-Without-Regrouping Method

```
  H T O
  7 3 9          O: Ones
−  3 2 5          T: Tens
-----------       H: Hundreds
  4 1 4
```

Since no regrouping is required, subtract the digits in each place value accordingly.

5. The Subtracting-by-Regrouping Method

```
  H T O
  5 ⁷8 ¹¹1        O: Ones
−  2 4 7          T: Tens
-----------       H: Hundreds
  3 3 4
```

In this example, students cannot subtract 7 ones from 1 one. So, regroup the tens and ones. Regroup 8 tens 1 one into 7 tens 11 ones.

6. The Subtracting-by-Regrouping-Twice Method

```
  H T O
 ⁷8 ⁹0 ¹⁰0        O: Ones
−  5 9 3          T: Tens
-----------       H: Hundreds
  2 0 7
```

In this example, students cannot subtract 3 ones from 0 ones and 9 tens from 0 tens. So, regroup the hundreds, tens, and ones. Regroup 8 hundreds into 7 hundreds 9 tens 10 ones.

7. The Multiplying-Without-Regrouping Method

```
  T O
  2 4          O: Ones
×   2          T: Tens
---------
  4 8
```

Since no regrouping is required, multiply the digit in each place value by the multiplier accordingly.

8. The Multiplying-With-Regrouping Method

```
  H T O
 ¹3 ²4 9          O: Ones
×      3          T: Tens
-----------       H: Hundreds
 1, 0 4 7
```

In this example, regroup 27 ones into 2 tens 7 ones, and 14 tens into 1 hundred 4 tens.

9. The Dividing-Without-Regrouping Method

```
        2 4 1
    2) 4 8 2
      −4
      -----
        8
       −8
       -----
         2
        −2
        -----
         0
```

Since no regrouping is required, divide the digit in each place value by the divisor accordingly.

10. The Dividing-With-Regrouping Method

```
        1 6 6
    5) 8 3 0
      −5
      -----
       3 3
      −3 0
      -----
         3 0
        −3 0
        -----
          0
```

In this example, regroup 3 hundreds into 30 tens and add 3 tens to make 33 tens. Regroup 3 tens into 30 ones.

11. The Addition-of-Fractions Method

$$\frac{1 \times 2}{6 \times 2} + \frac{1 \times 3}{4 \times 3} = \frac{2}{12} + \frac{3}{12} = \frac{5}{12}$$

Always remember to make the denominators common before adding the fractions.

12. The Subtraction-of-Fractions Method

$$\frac{1 \times 5}{2 \times 5} - \frac{1 \times 2}{5 \times 2} = \frac{5}{10} - \frac{2}{10} = \frac{3}{10}$$

Always remembers to make the denominators common before subtracting the fractions.

13. The Multiplication-of-Fractions Method

$$\frac{\cancel{3}^1}{5} \times \frac{1}{\cancel{9}_3} = \frac{1}{15}$$

When the numerator and the denominator have a common multiple, reduce them to their lowest fractions.

14. The Division-of-Fractions Method

$$\frac{7}{9} \div \frac{1}{6} = \frac{7}{\cancel{9}_3} \times \frac{\cancel{6}^2}{1} = \frac{14}{3} = 4\frac{2}{3}$$

When dividing fractions, first change the division sign (÷) to the multiplication sign (×). Then, switch the numerator and denominator of the fraction on the right hand side. Multiply the fractions in the usual way.

Model drawing is an effective strategy used to solve math word problems. It is a visual representation of the information in word problems using bar units. By drawing the models, students will know of the variables given in the problem, the variables to find, and even the methods used to solve the problem.

Drawing models is also a versatile strategy. It can be applied to simple word problems involving addition, subtraction, multiplication, and division. It can also be applied to word problems related to fractions, decimals, percentage, and ratio.

The use of models also trains students to think in an algebraic manner, which uses symbols for representation.

The different types of bar models used to solve word problems are illustrated below.

1. The model that involves addition

Melissa has 50 blue beads and 20 red beads. How many beads does she have altogether?

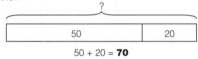

50 + 20 = **70**

2. The model that involves subtraction

Ben and Andy have 90 toy cars. Andy has 60 toy cars. How many toy cars does Ben have?

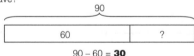

90 − 60 = **30**

3. The model that involves comparison

Mr. Simons has 150 magazines and 110 books in his study. How many more magazines than books does he have?

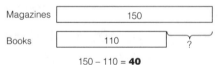

150 − 110 = **40**

4. The model that involves two items with a difference

A pair of shoes costs $109. A leather bag costs $241 more than the pair of shoes. How much is the leather bag?

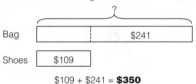

$109 + $241 = **$350**

Singapore Math Practice Level 2B

5. The model that involves multiples

Mrs. Drew buys 12 apples. She buys 3 times as many oranges as apples. She also buys 3 times as many cherries as oranges. How many pieces of fruit does she buy altogether?

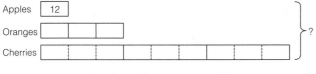

$$13 \times 12 = \textbf{156}$$

6. The model that involves multiples and difference

There are 15 students in Class A. There are 5 more students in Class B than in Class A. There are 3 times as many students in Class C than in Class A. How many students are there altogether in the three classes?

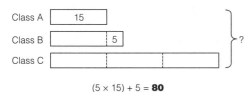

$$(5 \times 15) + 5 = \textbf{80}$$

7. The model that involves creating a whole

Ellen, Giselle, and Brenda bake 111 muffins. Giselle bakes twice as many muffins as Brenda. Ellen bakes 9 fewer muffins than Giselle. How many muffins does Ellen bake?

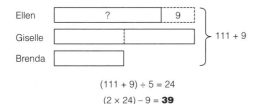

$$(111 + 9) \div 5 = 24$$
$$(2 \times 24) - 9 = \textbf{39}$$

8. The model that involves sharing

There are 183 tennis balls in Basket A and 97 tennis balls in Basket B. How many tennis balls must be transferred from Basket A to Basket B so that both baskets contain the same number of tennis balls?

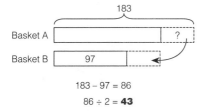

$$183 - 97 = 86$$
$$86 \div 2 = \textbf{43}$$

9. The model that involves fractions

George had 355 marbles. He lost $\frac{1}{5}$ of the marbles and gave $\frac{1}{4}$ of the remaining marbles to his brother. How many marbles did he have left?

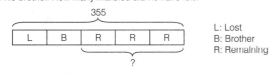

L: Lost
B: Brother
R: Remaining

5 parts → 355 marbles
1 part → 355 ÷ 5 = 71 marbles
3 parts → 3 × 71 = **213** marbles

10. The model that involves ratio

Aaron buys a tie and a belt. The prices of the tie and belt are in the ratio 2 : 5. If both items cost $539,

(a) what is the price of the tie?

(b) what is the price of the belt?

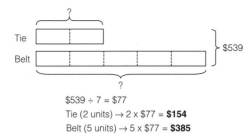

$$\$539 \div 7 = \$77$$
Tie (2 units) → 2 x $77 = **$154**
Belt (5 units) → 5 x $77 = **$385**

11. The model that involves comparison of fractions

Jack's height is $\frac{2}{3}$ of Leslie's height. Leslie's height is $\frac{3}{4}$ of Lindsay's height. If Lindsay is 160 cm tall, find Jack's height and Leslie's height.

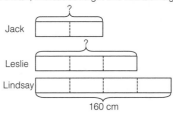

1 unit → 160 ÷ 4 = 40 cm

Leslie's height (3 units) → 3 × 40 = **120 cm**

Jack's height (2 units) → 2 × 40 = **80 cm**

Thinking skills and strategies are important in mathematical problem solving. These skills are applied when students think through the math problems to solve them. Below are some commonly used thinking skills and strategies applied in mathematical problem solving.

1. Comparing

Comparing is a form of thinking skill that students can apply to identify similarities and differences.

When comparing numbers, look carefully at each digit before deciding if a number is greater or less than the other. Students might also use a number line for comparison when there are more numbers.

Example:

3 is greater than 2 but smaller than 7.

2. Sequencing

A sequence shows the order of a series of numbers. *Sequencing* is a form of thinking skill that requires students to place numbers in a particular order. There are many terms in a sequence. The terms refer to the numbers in a sequence.

To place numbers in a correct order, students must first find a rule that generates the sequence. In a simple math sequence, students can either add or subtract to find the unknown terms in the sequence.

Example: Find the 7th term in the sequence below.

1,	4,	7,	10,	13,	16	?
1st term	2nd term	3rd term	4th term	5th term	6th term	7th term

Step 1:   This sequence is in an increasing order.

Step 2:   4 − 1 = 3   7 − 4 = 3
          The difference between two consecutive terms is 3.

Step 3:   16 + 3 = 19
          The 7th term is **19**.

3. Visualization

Visualization is a problem solving strategy that can help students visualize a problem through the use of physical objects. Students will play a more active role in solving the problem by manipulating these objects.

The main advantage of using this strategy is the mobility of information in the process of solving the problem. When students make a wrong step in the process, they can retrace the step without erasing or canceling it.

The other advantage is that this strategy helps develop a better understanding of the problem or solution through visual objects or images. In this way, students will be better able to remember how to solve these types of problems.

Some of the commonly used objects for this strategy are toothpicks, straws, cards, strings, water, sand, pencils, paper, and dice.

4. Look for a Pattern

This strategy requires the use of observational and analytical skills. Students have to observe the given data to find a pattern in order to solve the problem. Math word problems that involve the use of this strategy usually have repeated numbers or patterns.

Example: Find the sum of all the numbers from 1 to 100.

Step 1: <u>Simplify the problem.</u>
Find the sum of 1, 2, 3, 4, 5, 6, 7, 8, 9, and 10.

Step 2: <u>Look for a pattern.</u>

$1 + 10 = 11$	$2 + 9 = 11$	$3 + 8 = 11$
$4 + 7 = 11$	$5 + 6 = 11$	

Step 3: <u>Describe the pattern.</u>
When finding the sum of 1 to 10, add the first and last numbers to get a result of 11. Then, add the second and second last numbers to get the same result. The pattern continues until all the numbers from 1 to 10 are added. There will be 5 pairs of such results. Since each addition equals 11, the answer is then $5 \times 11 = 55$.

Step 4: <u>Use the pattern to find the answer.</u>
Since there are 5 pairs in the sum of 1 to 10, there should be ($10 \times 5 = 50$ pairs) in the sum of 1 to 100.
Note that the addition for each pair is not equal to 11 now. The addition for each pair is now ($1 + 100 = 101$).
$$50 \times 101 = 5050$$
The sum of all the numbers from 1 to 100 is **5,050**.

5. Working Backward

The strategy of working backward applies only to a specific type of math word problem. These word problems state the end result, and students are required to find the total number. In order to solve these word problems, students have to work backward by thinking through the correct sequence of events. The strategy of working backward allows students to use their logical reasoning and sequencing to find the answers.

Example: Sarah has a piece of ribbon. She cuts the ribbon into 4 equal parts. Each part is then cut into 3 smaller equal parts. If the length of each small part is 35 cm, how long is the piece of ribbon?
$$3 \times 35 = 105 \text{ cm}$$
$$4 \times 105 = 420 \text{ cm}$$
The piece of ribbon is **420 cm**.

6. The Before-After Concept

The *Before-After* concept lists all the relevant data before and after an event. Students can then compare the differences and eventually solve the problems. Usually, the Before-After concept and the mathematical model go hand in hand to solve math word problems. Note that the Before-After concept can be applied only to a certain type of math word problem, which trains students to think sequentially.

Example: Kelly has 4 times as much money as Joey. After Kelly uses some money to buy a tennis racquet, and Joey uses $30 to buy a pair of pants, Kelly has twice as much money as Joey. If Joey has $98 in the beginning,
(a) how much money does Kelly have in the end?
(b) how much money does Kelly spend on the tennis racquet?

Before

Kelly

Joey $98

After

Kelly

Joey $30

(a) $98 - $30 = $68
$2 \times $68 = 136
Kelly has **$136** in the end.

(b) $4 \times $98 = 392
$392 - $136 = $256
Kelly spends **$256** on the tennis racquet.

7. Making Supposition

Making supposition is commonly known as "making an assumption." Students can use this strategy to solve certain types of math word problems. Making

assumptions will eliminate some possibilities and simplifies the word problems by providing a boundary of values to work within.

Example: Mrs. Jackson bought 100 pieces of candy for all the students in her class. How many pieces of candy would each student receive if there were 25 students in her class?

In the above word problem, assume that each student received the same number of pieces. This eliminates the possibilities that some students would receive more than others due to good behaviour, better results, or any other reason.

8. Representation of Problem

In problem solving, students often use representations in the solutions to show their understanding of the problems. Using representations also allow students to understand the mathematical concepts and relationships as well as to manipulate the information presented in the problems. Examples of representations are diagrams and lists or tables.

Diagrams allow students to consolidate or organize the information given in the problems. By drawing a diagram, students can see the problem clearly and solve it effectively.

A list or table can help students organize information that is useful for analysis. After analyzing, students can then see a pattern, which can be used to solve the problem.

9. Guess and Check

One of the most important and effective problem-solving techniques is *Guess and Check*. It is also known as *Trial and Error*. As the name suggests, students have to guess the answer to a problem and check if that guess is correct. If the guess is wrong, students will make another guess. This will continue until the guess is correct.

It is beneficial to keep a record of all the guesses and checks in a table. In addition, a *Comments* column can be included. This will enable students to analyze their guess (if it is too high or too low) and improve on the next guess. Be careful; this problem-solving technique can be tiresome without systematic or logical guesses.

Example: Jessica had 15 coins. Some of them were 10-cent coins and the rest were 5-cent coins. The total amount added up to $1.25. How many coins of each kind were there?

Use the guess-and-check method.

Number of 10¢ Coins	Value	Number of 5¢ Coins	Value	Total Number of Coins	Total Value
7	$7 \times 10¢ = 70¢$	8	$8 \times 5¢ = 40¢$	$7 + 8 = 15$	70¢ + 40¢ = 110¢ = $1.10
8	$8 \times 10¢ = 80¢$	7	$7 \times 5¢ = 35¢$	$8 + 7 = 15$	80¢ + 35¢ = 115¢ = $1.15
10	$10 \times 10¢ = 100¢$	5	$5 \times 5¢ = 25¢$	$10 + 5 = 15$	100¢ + 25¢ = 125¢ = $1.25

There were **ten** 10-cent coins and **five** 5-cent coins.

10. Restate the Problem

When solving challenging math problems, conventional methods may not be workable. Instead, restating the problem will enable students to see some challenging problems in a different light so that they can better understand them.

The strategy of restating the problem is to "say" the problem in a different and clearer way. However, students have to ensure that the main idea of the problem is not altered.

How do students restate a math problem?

First, read and understand the problem. Gather the given facts and unknowns. Note any condition(s) that have to be satisfied.

Next, restate the problem. Imagine narrating this problem to a friend. Present the given facts, unknown(s), and condition(s). Students may want to write the "revised" problem. Once the "revised" problem is analyzed, students should be able to think of an appropriate strategy to solve it.

11. Simplify the Problem

One of the commonly used strategies in mathematical problem solving is simplification of the problem. When a problem is simplified, it can be "broken down" into two or more smaller parts. Students can then solve the parts systematically to get to the final answer.

6

Table of Contents

Singapore Math Practice Level 2B

LEARNING OUTCOMES

Unit 10 Mental Calculations

Students should be able to
- add 2 numbers mentally.
- subtract 2 numbers mentally.

Unit 11 Money

Students should be able to
- count and write money in dollars and cents.
- convert dollars to cents or cents to dollars.
- compare money.
- solve story problems related to money.

Review 1

This review tests students' understanding of Units 10 & 11.

Unit 12 Fractions

Students should be able to
- understand that fractions are equal parts.
- identify fractions from $\frac{1}{2}$ to $\frac{1}{12}$.
- compare and arrange fractions.
- add and subtract like fractions.
- solve story problems related to fractions.

Unit 13 Time

Students should be able to
- read and write the correct time.
- use *A.M.*, *P.M.*, *hr.*, and *min.* correctly.
- draw hour and minute hands correctly.
- find the time half an hour or one hour before/after a certain time.

Review 2

This review tests students' understanding of Units 12 & 13.

Unit 14 Volume

Students should be able to

- compare volumes of liquid.
- read and measure volumes of liquid in liters and gallons.
- add, subtract, multiply, and divide volume.
- solve story problems related to volume.

Unit 15 Graphs

Students should be able to
- read and understand picture graphs with scales.
- create picture graphs with scales.
- use picture graphs to solve problems.

Review 3

This review tests students' understanding of Units 14 & 15.

Unit 16 Lines and Surfaces

Students should be able to
- recognize straight lines and curves.
- recognize objects with only flat surfaces.
- count the number of flat surfaces an object has.

Unit 17 Shapes and Patterns

Students should be able to
- recognize squares, rectangles, circles, semicircles, quarter circles, and triangles in 2-D objects.
- recognize cubes, cuboids, cones, and cylinders in 3-D objects.
- draw 2-D shapes on dot or square grids.
- complete a pattern.

Review 4

This review tests students' understanding of Units 16 & 17.

Final Review

This review is an excellent assessment of students' understanding of all the topics in this book.

Singapore Math Practice Level 2B

FORMULA SHEET

Unit 10 Mental Calculations

Addition and subtraction can be done mentally by rounding numbers and breaking up numbers.

Mental addition by rounding numbers
① Round one of the addends, A, to the nearest ten.
② Mentally add the rounded number to the other addend, B.
③ Subtract the difference between the rounded number and addend A from the sum.

Mental addition by breaking up numbers
When one of the addends, A, is less than 10,
① break up the other addend, B, into ones and tens/hundreds.
Example: Break up 364 into 4 and 360.
② Add the ones to get a sum.
③ Add the sum to the remaining tens/hundreds to get the final answer.
Apply the same method to an addend that is less than 100 or 1,000.

Mental subtraction by rounding numbers
① Round one of the subtrahends, A, to the nearest ten.
② Mentally subtract the rounded number from the other subtrahend, B.
③ Add the difference between the rounded number and subtrahend A to the result in ②.

Mental subtraction by breaking up numbers
When one of the subtrahends, A, is less than 10,
① break up the other subtrahend, B, into ones and tens/hundreds.
Example: Break up 526 into 6 and 520.
② Subtract the ones to get a result.
③ Add the result in ② to the remaining tens/hundreds.
Apply the same method to a subtrahend that is less than 100 or 1,000.

Unit 11 Money

Writing dollars and cents
$1 = 100¢
When writing dollars and cents, place a dollar sign ($) in the front and a decimal point (.) to separate them.
Example: $8.95
When writing dollars without any cents, add 2 zeros after the decimal point.
Example: $8.00
When writing cents without any dollars, add a zero before the decimal point.
Example: $0.95

Converting dollars to cents
• Remove the dollar sign ($) and the decimal point (.).
• Place the cent symbol (¢) after the number.
Example: $20.50 = 2,050¢

Converting cents to dollars
• Remove the cent symbol (¢).
• Place the dollar sign ($) before the number.
• Place the decimal point (.) just before the last 2 digits.
Example: 3,000¢ = $30.00

Comparing money
• Compare the dollars of the 2 amounts first.
• If the dollars are the same, compare the cents.

Unit 12 Fractions

In a fraction, each part must be equal.
Examples of a fraction: $\frac{1}{2}$, $\frac{2}{5}$, and $\frac{8}{8}$.
To make a whole, make sure all denominators are common. All numerators add up to equal the denominator.
Example: $\frac{2}{8}$ and $\frac{6}{8}$ make a whole.

Comparing and arranging fractions in order
• When denominators of all fractions are the same, compare their numerators.
  The largest fraction has the highest value in the numerator.
  Example: $\underset{\text{largest}}{\frac{4}{5}}$, $\frac{2}{5}$, $\frac{1}{5}$
• When numerators of all fractions are the same, compare their denominators.
  The largest fraction has the smallest value in the denominator.
  Example: $\underset{\text{largest}}{\frac{1}{4}}$, $\frac{1}{8}$, $\frac{1}{12}$

This table can be useful when comparing fractions.

Singapore Math Practice Level 2B

Adding and subtracting fractions
- Make sure denominators of all fractions are the same.
- Add and subtract the numerators accordingly.

When one of the subtrahends is a whole, convert the whole into a fraction before subtracting.

Unit 13 Time

There are 24 hours in a day.

1 hour = 60 minutes

Numbers 1 to 12 can be seen on the face of a clock, as well as the hour hand and minute hand.

The minute hand is longer than the hour hand.

When the minute hand moves from one number to another, 5 minutes has passed.

When the hour hand moves from one number to another, 1 hour has passed.

The units of measurement for time are hour (hr.) and minute (min.).

Writing and reading time

We read the time on the clock as three twenty-five.

We write it as 3:25.

The abbreviation *A.M.* means before noon and *P.M.* means after noon.

Hence *A.M.* is used to talk about time between 12 midnight and 11:59 in the morning.

P.M. is used to talk about time between 12 noon and 11:59 at night.

We can find the time before/after a certain time if the duration is given.

Examples: 10:00 A.M. is 1 hr. before 11:00 A.M.
  7:00 P.M. is 1 hr. after 6:00 P.M.
  9:30 A.M. is 30 min. before 10:00 A.M.
  5:30 P.M. is 30 min. after 5:00 P.M.

Unit 14 Volume

The volume of water in a container is the amount of water the container holds.

Comparing volume
- When the water level in 2 identical containers is the same, use the words *as much as*.
- When the water level in one container is higher than that of the other container, use the words *more than*.
- When the water level in one container is lower than that of the other container, use the words *less than*.

The unit of measurement for volume is liter (L) or gallon (gal.).

Unit 15 Graphs

Symbols represent the items in picture graphs.

Note the scales used in picture graphs. The symbol can stand for 1 item, 2 items, or even more.

Picture graphs help organize information for easy interpretation and problem solving.

Unit 16 Lines and Surfaces

Examples of straight lines:

Examples of curves:

Examples of items with only flat surfaces:

Unit 17 Shapes and Patterns

2-dimensional shapes and objects

Examples of different shapes:

square rectangle triangle circle semicircle quarter circle

These shapes can be used to create a 2-dimensional figure.

An example of a 2-dimensional figure that is made of 2 quarter circles, a square, and a triangle.

3-dimensional objects

Examples of 3-dimensional objects:

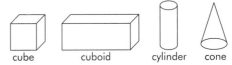

cube cuboid cylinder cone

These shapes can be used to create a 3-dimensional figure.

An example of a 3-dimensional figure that is made of 2 cubes and a cylinder.

Patterns

Shapes can be used to create a repeated pattern.

An example of a repeated pattern using different shapes:

An example of a repeated pattern using different sizes:

An example of a repeated pattern using different colors:

Singapore Math Practice Level 2B

Unit 10: MENTAL CALCULATIONS

Examples:

1. What is 69 + 7?

    69 + 10 = 79

    79 – 3 = 76

    69 + 7 = **76**

2. What is 364 + 5?

    364 = 360 + 4

    4 + 5 = 9

    360 + 9 = 369

    364 + 5 = **369**

3. What is 158 + 30?

    158 = 108 + 50

    50 + 30 = 80

    108 + 80 = 188

    158 + 30 = **188**

4. What is 592 + 400?

    592 = 500 + 92

    500 + 400 = 900

    900 + 92 = 992

    592 + 400 = **992**

5. What is 95 – 9?

    95 – 10 = 85

    85 + 1 = 86

    95 – 9 = **86**

6. What is 438 – 60?

    438 – 100 = 338

    338 + 40 = 378

    438 – 60 = **378**

7. What is 247 – 40?

    247 = 207 + 40

    40 – 40 = 0

    207 + 0 = 207

    247 – 40 = **207**

8. What is 689 – 300?

    689 = 600 + 89

    600 – 300 = 300

    300 + 89 = 389

    689 – 300 = **389**

Solve the following addition problems mentally.

1. 64 + 8 = _____

2. 89 + 7 = _____

3. 26 + 5 = _____

4. 18 + 9 = _____

5. 57 + 6 = _____

6. 45 + 8 = _____

7. 37 + 5 = _____

8. 78 + 8 = _____

9. 94 + 9 = _____

10. 56 + 7 = _____

11. 127 + 5 = _____

12. 764 + 9 = _____

13. 262 + 6 = _____

14. 948 + 8 = _____

15. 435 + 7 = _____

16. 584 + 6 = _____

17. 623 + 9 = _____

18. 806 + 9 = _____

19. 366 + 5 = _____

20. 119 + 6 = _____

Singapore Math Practice Level 2B

21. 513 + 6 = _____

22. 836 + 20 = _____

23. 723 + 80 = _____

24. 190 + 70 = _____

25. 428 + 40 = _____

26. 762 + 70 = _____

27. 503 + 90 = _____

28. 869 + 80 = _____

29. 623 + 60 = _____

30. 770 + 200 = _____

31. 323 + 600 = _____

32. 165 + 800 = _____

33. 248 + 500 = _____

34. 657 + 300 = _____

35. 195 + 700 = _____

36. 108 + 200 = _____

37. 588 + 400 = _____

38. 645 + 100 = _____

39. 199 + 600 = _____

40. 756 + 200 = _____

Singapore Math Practice Level 2B

Solve the following subtraction problems mentally.

41. $52 - 5 = $ _____

42. $46 - 9 = $ _____

43. $81 - 8 = $ _____

44. $30 - 7 = $ _____

45. $88 - 3 = $ _____

46. $79 - 5 = $ _____

47. $64 - 4 = $ _____

48. $28 - 9 = $ _____

49. $93 - 1 = $ _____

50. $59 - 7 = $ _____

51. $620 - 5 = $ _____

52. $404 - 6 = $ _____

53. $875 - 4 = $ _____

54. $740 - 2 = $ _____

55. $519 - 9 = $ _____

56. $264 - 7 = $ _____

57. $329 - 6 = $ _____

58. $183 - 5 = $ _____

59. $916 - 3 = $ _____

60. $534 - 8 = $ _____

61. 415 – 30 = _____

62. 338 – 90 = _____

63. 587 – 60 = _____

64. 860 – 50 = _____

65. 609 – 10 = _____

66. 281 – 20 = _____

67. 758 – 40 = _____

68. 495 – 70 = _____

69. 164 – 80 = _____

70. 626 – 60 = _____

71. 758 – 300 = _____

72. 834 – 600 = _____

73. 905 – 800 = _____

74. 631 – 500 = _____

75. 978 – 900 = _____

76. 505 – 100 = _____

77. 784 – 400 = _____

78. 435 – 200 = _____

79. 876 – 700 = _____

80. 980 – 800 = _____

Unit 11: MONEY

1. Andy receives a sum of money from his parents.
    How much does Andy receive?

$10	$1	50¢
$5	$1	$1

    Andy receives **$18.50**.

2. Change $3.95 to cents.

    $3.95 = **395¢**

3. Change 1,000¢ to dollars.

    1,000¢ = **$10.00**

4. Natalie spent $12.60 on food.
    Sammi spent $15.60, and Omar spent $20.90.
    Who spent the most money?

    Among the 3 amounts, $20.90 is the greatest.

    Omar spent the most money.

Singapore Math Practice Level 2B

1. Write the correct amount of money in numerals.

    (a) ten dollars   _____

    (b) two dollars and fifty cents   _____

    (c) forty-four dollars and forty cents   _____

    (d) thirty-nine dollars and eighty-five cents   _____

    (e) sixty-seven dollars and ninety cents   _____

    (f) fifty dollars and five cents   _____

    (g) nineteen dollars and seventy cents   _____

    (h) eighty-seven cents   _____

    (i) twelve dollars and fifteen cents   _____

    (j) twenty dollars and twenty-five cents   _____

2. Write the amount of money in words.

    (a) $12.30 = _____ dollars and _____ cents

    (b) $45.45 = _____ dollars and _____ cents

    (c) $67.05 = _____ dollars and _____ cents

    (d) $15.55 = _____ dollars and _____ cents

    (e) $ 7.90 = _____ dollars and _____ cents

    (f) $11.80 = _____ dollars and _____ cents

    (g) $36.60 = _____ dollars and _____ cents

    (h) $20.15 = _____ dollars and _____ cents

    (i) $59.95 = _____ dollars and _____ cents

    (j) $70.70 = _____ dollars and _____ cents

Write the correct amount of money on the lines provided.

3.

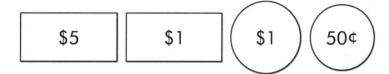

_____¢

4.

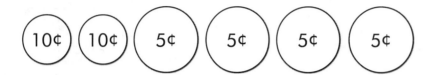

$_____

5.

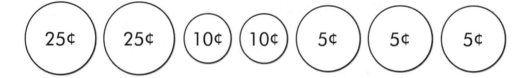

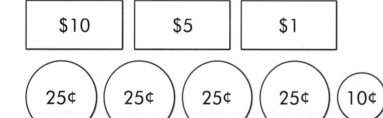

$_____

6.

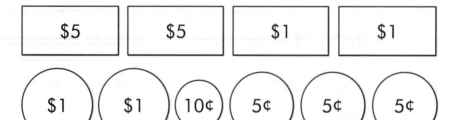

$_____

7.

$5 $5 $1 $1

$1 $1   10¢   5¢   5¢   5¢

$_____

Singapore Math Practice Level 2B

The amount of money each item costs is shown below. Write the correct amount of money on the lines provided.

8.

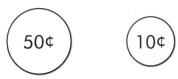

An eraser costs _____.

9.

A book costs _____.

10.

A bag of birdseed costs _____.

11.

A set of colored pencils costs _____.

12.

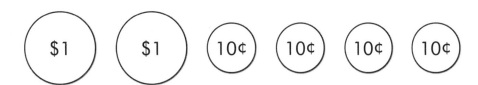

A notebook costs _____.

Singapore Math Practice Level 2B

13. Write the following amounts in cents.

   (a) $2.25 = _____ ¢   (f) $89.05 = _____ ¢

   (b) $10.50 = _____ ¢   (g) $100.30 = _____ ¢

   (c) $35.75 = _____ ¢   (h) $40.40 = _____ ¢

   (d) $50.05 = _____ ¢   (i) $15.95 = _____ ¢

   (e) $27.35 = _____ ¢   (j) $20.55 = _____ ¢

14. Write the following amounts in dollars.

   (a) 416¢ = $_____   (f) 960¢ = $_____

   (b) 1,875¢ = $_____   (g) 1,005¢ = $_____

   (c) 3,005¢ = $_____   (h) 7,600¢ = $_____

   (d) 805¢ = $_____   (i) 18¢ = $_____

   (e) 1,750¢ = $_____   (j) 59¢ = $_____

Fill in each blank with the correct answer.

15. Christopher spends $26.50 in a week.
    George spends $32.50 in a week.

   (a) $_____ is more than $_____.

   (b) _____ spends more money.

16. Marcos saves $55.85 in a month.
    Noelle saves $45.90 in a month.

   (a) $_____ is less than $_____.

   (b) _____ saves more money.

Singapore Math Practice Level 2B

17. Mrs. Adams has $67.80.
    Mrs. Morales has $65.90.

    (a) $_____ is more than $_____.

    (b) $_____ is less than $_____.

    (c) _____ has less money.

18. Samira's weekly allowance is $26.50.
    Kate's weekly allowance is $19.60.
    Lucy's weekly allowance is $23.25.

    (a) $_____ is the smallest amount of money.

    (b) $_____ is the largest amount of money.

    (c) _____ has the most weekly allowance.

    (d) _____ has the least weekly allowance.

Solve the following story problems. Show your work in the space below.

19. A book costs $3. Malia bought 6 books. How much did she pay for the books?

    She paid _____ for the books.

Singapore Math Practice Level 2B

20. A peach costs 55¢. A banana costs 25¢ less than the peach. What is the total cost of the peach and the banana?

The total cost of the peach and the banana is _____.

21. Aunt Rose earns $350 in a week. Uncle James earns $190 more per week than Aunt Rose. How much money do both of them earn in a week?

Both of them earn _____ in a week.

22. Gina bought a doll for $29. She gave the cashier $100. How much change did she receive?

She received _____ in change.

23. Mr. Singh gives his son $40 every 10 days. If his son spends an equal amount of money every day, how much money does he spend per day?

He spends _____ per day.

REVIEW 1

Fill in each blank with the correct answer.

1. Write ninety-nine dollars and nine cents in numerals.   _____

2. Add 814 and 90 mentally.   _____

3. $55.15 = _____ dollars and _____ cents

4. How much money is shown below?

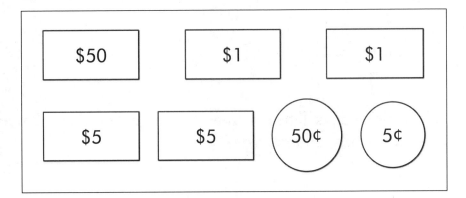

_____

5. Write $62.85 in cents.   _____

6. Add 604 and 200 mentally.   _____

7. Grace has $30.05. Jerome has $35.55.

    (a) $_____ is more than $_____.

    (b) _____ has more money.

8. Subtract 9 from 546 mentally.   _____

Singapore Math Practice Level 2B

9. Write 3,840¢ in dollars. _____

10. Subtract 60 from 743 mentally. _____

11.

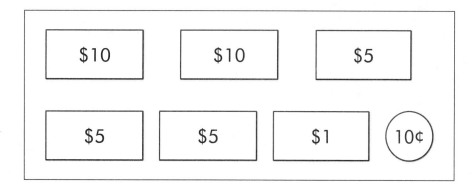

A purse costs _____.

12. Uncle Sam pays $45 for a bouquet of roses.
Uncle Rafael pays $42 for a bouquet of sunflowers.

(a) $_____ is less than $_____.

(b) _____ pays more for the flowers.

13. $100.10 = _____ dollars and _____ cents

14. Add 5 and 686 mentally. _____

15. Subtract 400 from 712 mentally. _____

Singapore Math Practice Level 2B

Solve the following story problems. Show your work in the space below.

16. Emma saves $2 each day. How much money does she save in a week?

    Emma saves _____ in a week.

17. Samantha bought a calculator. She gave the cashier $50 and received $2 in change. How much did the calculator cost?

    The calculator cost _____.

18. Vera bought a dress for $49. She bought a shirt for $35. How much money did she spend in all?

She spent _____ in all.

19. Uncle Ronald gives some money to his 3 children. Each child receives $7. How much money does Uncle Ronald give to his children in all?

Uncle Ronald gives _____ to his children in all.

20. Natasha pays $60 for 6 identical towels. How much does each towel cost?

Each towel costs _____.

Unit 12: FRACTIONS

Examples:

1. Arrange $\frac{3}{7}$, $\frac{1}{7}$, and $\frac{5}{7}$ in order, beginning with the smallest.

$$\underline{\frac{1}{7},\qquad\frac{3}{7},\qquad\frac{5}{7}}$$
smallest

2. Add $\frac{2}{9}$ and $\frac{5}{9}$.

$$\frac{2}{9} + \frac{5}{9} = \underline{\frac{7}{9}}$$

3. What is $1 - \frac{5}{6}$?

$$1 - \frac{5}{6} = \frac{6}{6} - \frac{5}{6} = \underline{\frac{1}{6}}$$

4. Lexi used $\frac{3}{8}$ of the butter in the morning. She used $\frac{4}{8}$ of the butter in the afternoon. What fraction of the butter did Lexi use altogether?

| M | M | M | A | A | A | A | |

M: Morning
A: Afternoon

$$\frac{3}{8} + \frac{4}{8} = \frac{7}{8}$$

Lexi used $\underline{\frac{7}{8}}$ of the butter altogether.

Singapore Math Practice Level 2B

Put a check mark (✓) in the box if the shape is divided into equal parts.

1.

3.

2.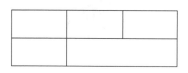

4.

What fraction of each figure is shaded? Write the correct answer on the line.

5.  _____

8. 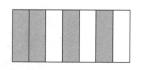 _____

6. 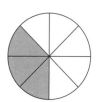 _____

9. 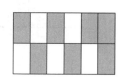 _____

7. 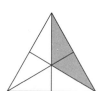 _____

Singapore Math Practice Level 2B

Shade the parts of each figure to show the correct fractions.

10. $\frac{2}{3}$

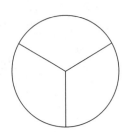

11. $\frac{4}{9}$

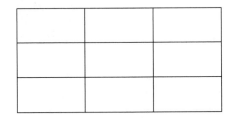

12. $\frac{5}{11}$

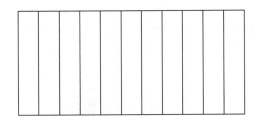

13. $\frac{6}{8}$

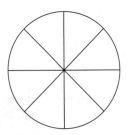

14. $\frac{5}{6}$

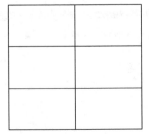

Singapore Math Practice Level 2B

Fill in each blank with the correct answer.

15.

(a) _____ parts of the figure are shaded.

(b) There are _____ equal parts altogether.

(c) _____ of the figure is shaded.

(d) _____ of the figure is not shaded.

16.

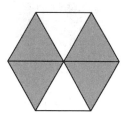

(a) _____ parts of the figure are shaded.

(b) There are _____ equal parts altogether.

(c) The fraction of the figure that is shaded is _____.

(d) The fraction of the figure that is not shaded is _____.

17.

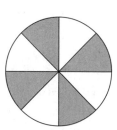

(a) _____ out of _____ equal parts are shaded.

(b) _____ of the figure is shaded.

Singapore Math Practice Level 2B

18.

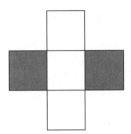

(a) _____ out of _____ equal parts are shaded.

(b) _____ of the figure is shaded.

19.

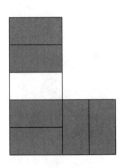

(a) _____ out of _____ equal parts are shaded.

(b) _____ of the figure is shaded.

20. Lisa cuts a cake into 8 equal parts. Her brother eats 2 parts.

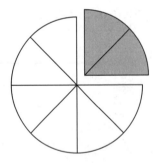

(a) _____ parts of the cake are left.

(b) The fraction of the cake that her brother eats is _____.

(c) The fraction of the cake left is _____.

(d) _____ and _____ make a whole.

Singapore Math Practice Level 2B

21. Hiroshi cuts a loaf of bread into 5 equal parts. He eats 3 parts.

(a) _____ parts of the bread are left.

(b) The fraction of the bread that Hiroshi eats is _____.

(c) The fraction of the bread left is _____.

(d) _____ and _____ make a whole.

Fill in each blank with the correct answer.

22. _____ and $\frac{1}{3}$ make a whole.

23. _____ and $\frac{1}{2}$ make a whole.

24. $\frac{3}{7}$ and _____ make a whole.

25. _____ and $\frac{4}{11}$ make a whole.

26. _____ and $\frac{9}{12}$ make a whole.

27. $\frac{2}{5}$ and _____ make a whole.

28. $\frac{6}{8}$ and _____ make a whole.

29. $\frac{3}{9}$ and _____ make a whole.

30. _____ and $\frac{1}{4}$ make a whole.

31. _____ and $\frac{1}{6}$ make a whole.

Singapore Math Practice Level 2B

Circle the larger fraction in each pair.

32.

$$\frac{1}{2}$$

$$\frac{1}{4}$$

33.

$$\frac{3}{8}$$

$$\frac{3}{6}$$

34.

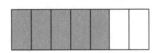

$$\frac{5}{7}$$

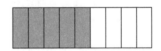

$$\frac{5}{9}$$

Circle the smaller fraction in each pair.

35.

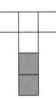

$$\frac{2}{6}$$

$$\frac{2}{4}$$

36.

$$\frac{1}{3}$$

$$\frac{1}{5}$$

Singapore Math Practice Level 2B

37. 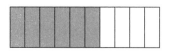　　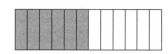

$$\frac{6}{10}$$　　　　　　　$$\frac{6}{12}$$

Color the correct part(s) of each figure to show the fractions. Then, circle the largest fraction in each set.

38.　$\frac{1}{8}$

　　$\frac{3}{8}$

　　$\frac{5}{8}$

39.　$\frac{2}{6}$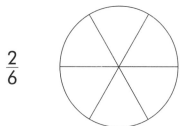

　　$\frac{2}{8}$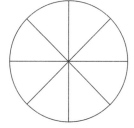

　　$\frac{2}{10}$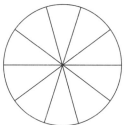

Singapore Math Practice Level 2B

40.
$\frac{1}{4}$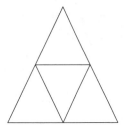

$\frac{2}{4}$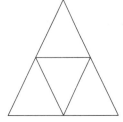

$\frac{3}{4}$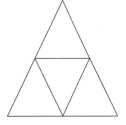

Color the part(s) of each figure to show the fractions. Then, circle the smaller fraction in each pair.

41.
$\frac{3}{9}$

$\frac{2}{9}$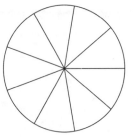

42. $\dfrac{4}{5}$

$\dfrac{4}{8}$

43. $\dfrac{8}{10}$

$\dfrac{6}{10}$

Circle the smaller fraction in each pair.

44. $\dfrac{1}{5}$ $\dfrac{1}{3}$

45. $\dfrac{2}{6}$ $\dfrac{2}{8}$

46. $\dfrac{4}{8}$ $\dfrac{3}{8}$

Circle the larger fraction in each pair.

47. $\dfrac{2}{3}$ $\dfrac{1}{3}$

48. $\dfrac{4}{8}$ $\dfrac{4}{5}$

49. $\dfrac{7}{10}$ $\dfrac{7}{11}$

Circle the largest fraction in each set.

50. $\dfrac{3}{5}$ $\dfrac{4}{5}$ $\dfrac{5}{5}$

51. $\dfrac{1}{10}$ $\dfrac{1}{11}$ $\dfrac{1}{12}$

52. $\dfrac{5}{7}$ $\dfrac{5}{8}$ $\dfrac{5}{9}$

Circle the smallest fraction in each set.

53. $\dfrac{1}{3}$ $\dfrac{1}{4}$ $\dfrac{1}{5}$

54. $\dfrac{7}{7}$ $\dfrac{4}{7}$ $\dfrac{5}{7}$

55. $\dfrac{5}{9}$ $\dfrac{6}{9}$ $\dfrac{3}{9}$

Singapore Math Practice Level 2B

Arrange the fractions in each set. Begin with the largest.

56.

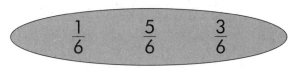

_____, _____, _____
largest

57.

_____, _____, _____
largest

58.

_____, _____, _____
largest

Arrange the fractions in each set. Begin with the smallest.

59.

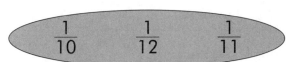

_____, _____, _____
smallest

60.

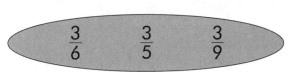

_____, _____, _____
smallest

Singapore Math Practice Level 2B

61.

_____, _____, _____
smallest

Add these fractions.

62. $\frac{1}{8} + \frac{2}{8}$ = _____

63. $\frac{1}{10} + \frac{6}{10}$ = _____

64. $\frac{3}{12} + \frac{7}{12}$ = _____

65. $\frac{2}{7} + \frac{4}{7}$ = _____

66. $\frac{1}{9} + \frac{5}{9} + \frac{2}{9}$ = _____

67. $\frac{1}{5} + \frac{2}{5} + \frac{1}{5}$ = _____

68. $\frac{2}{6} + \frac{1}{6} + \frac{1}{6}$ = _____

69. $\frac{2}{11} + \frac{1}{11} + \frac{3}{11}$ = _____

Subtract these fractions.

70. $\frac{3}{4} - \frac{1}{4}$ = _____

71. $\frac{5}{9} - \frac{3}{9}$ = _____

72. $\frac{6}{7} - \frac{1}{7}$ = _____

73. $1 - \frac{1}{10}$ = _____

74. $\frac{5}{6} - \frac{1}{6} - \frac{2}{6}$ = _____

75. $\frac{10}{11} - \frac{3}{11} - \frac{4}{11}$ = _____

76. $\frac{6}{8} - \frac{1}{8} - \frac{2}{8}$ = _____

77. $\frac{10}{12} - \frac{2}{12} - \frac{5}{12}$ = _____

Singapore Math Practice Level 2B

Solve the following story problems. Show your work in the space below.

78. Benny cuts a loaf of bread into 5 parts. His sister eats 2 pieces of the bread. What fraction of the bread is left?

_____ of the bread is left.

79. Mom eats $\frac{1}{10}$ of a pizza. Dad eats $\frac{3}{10}$ of the pizza. Kaylee eats $\frac{1}{10}$ of the pizza. What fraction of the pizza have they eaten?

They have eaten _____ of the pizza.

Singapore Math Practice Level 2B

80. Ileana used $\frac{1}{7}$ of her weekly allowance to buy a pencil case. She used another $\frac{3}{7}$ of it to buy some drawing materials. What fraction of her weekly allowance did she use?

She used _____ of her weekly allowance.

81. Aunt Carol made a pitcher of orange juice. Her children drank $\frac{3}{8}$ of the orange juice. What fraction of the pitcher of orange juice was left?

_____ of the pitcher of orange juice was left.

82. $\frac{1}{6}$ of the people at a party are children. $\frac{3}{6}$ of the people are women. The remaining people are men. What fraction of the people at the party are children and women?

_____ of the people at the party are children and women.

Singapore Math Practice Level 2B

Unit 13: TIME

Examples:

1. Write the time shown on the clock.

   The time is **6:20**.

2. Kelly eats her lunch 1 hour after noon. Write <u>A.M.</u> or <u>P.M.</u> in the blank.

   She eats her lunch at 1:00 **P.M.**

3. Henry took a bus to the zoo at 11:00 A.M. He reached the zoo 30 minutes later. At what time did he reach the zoo?

   He reached the zoo at **11:30 A.M.**

1. Look at the clock below. Fill in each box with the correct answer.

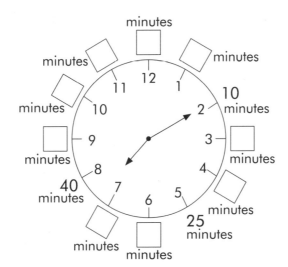

The time shown on the clock is _____ A.M.

Singapore Math Practice Level 2B

What time is it? Write the correct minutes on the lines below.

2.

_____ minutes after 8 o'clock

4.

_____ minutes after 6 o'clock

3.

_____ minutes after 4 o'clock

5.

_____ minutes after 7 o'clock

Write the correct time on the lines below.

6.

The time is _____.

8.

The time is _____.

7.

The time is _____.

9.

The time is _____.

Singapore Math Practice Level 2B

Match each clock to the correct time.

10.  •

• 3:10

11.  •

• 5:20

12.  •

• 9:35

13.  •

• 11:05

14.  •

• 7:55

Singapore Math Practice Level 2B

Draw the minute hand on each clock.

15.

The time is 4:15.

16.

The time is 6:00.

17.

The time is 11:30.

18.

The time is 1:45.

19.

The time is 2:10.

20.

The time is 8:55.

21.

The time is 9:05.

22.

The time is 3:50.

Singapore Math Practice Level 2B

Read the time, and draw the hour and minute hands on each clock.

23.

The time is 1:20.

27.

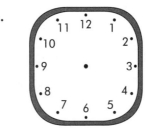

The time is 5:00.

24.

The time is 10:30.

28.

The time is 9:25.

25.

The time is 11:15.

29.

The time is 6:45.

26.

The time is 3:55.

30.

The time is 7:10.

Singapore Math Practice Level 2B

Fill in each blank with *A.M.* or *P.M.*

31. Pilar eats her breakfast
    at 8:00 _____.

32. The class will end at 12:50 _____.

33. Claire likes to take her dog for
    a walk after dinner. She usually
    gets home at 9:00 _____.

34. Mrs. Thomas goes to the grocery store
    after preparing breakfast. She leaves
    her house at 10:00 _____.

35. Braden and his family enjoy watching
    the evening news. The news will
    start at 9:30 _____.

Singapore Math Practice Level 2B

Fill in each blank with the correct answer.

36.

_____ is 30 min. after _____

37.

_____ is 30 min. after _____

38.

_____ is 1 hr. after _____

39.

_____ is 3 hr. before _____

40.

_____ is 4 hr. before _____

Singapore Math Practice Level 2B

Draw the time on each clock. Fill in each blank with the correct answer.

41.

    10:30 A.M. is 30 min. before _____.

42.

    8:00 P.M. is 1 hr. after _____.

43.

    5:30 A.M. is 30 min. after _____.

44.

    3:30 P.M. is 30 min. before _____.

45.

    1:00 P.M. is 1 hr. after _____.

Singapore Math Practice Level 2B

REVIEW 2

1. Which of the following are fractions? Put a check mark (✓) in the correct boxes.

    (a)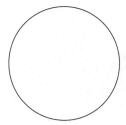

    (c)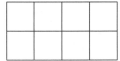

    (b)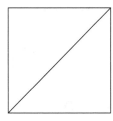

Shade the parts of each figure to show the fractions.

2. $\dfrac{5}{6}$

3. $\dfrac{6}{10}$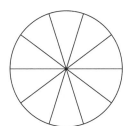

Singapore Math Practice Level 2B

Write the correct times on the lines below.

4.

_____

6.

_____

5.

_____

7.

_____

Draw the minute hand on each clock to show the correct time.

8.

3:45

10.

9:00

9.

2:15

11.

6:50

Singapore Math Practice Level 2B

Arrange the fractions in each set. Begin with the largest.

12.

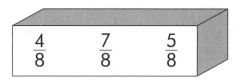

$\frac{5}{7}$ $\frac{1}{7}$ $\frac{6}{7}$

————— , ————— , —————
largest

Arrange the fractions in each set. Begin with the smallest.

13.

$\frac{4}{8}$ $\frac{7}{8}$ $\frac{5}{8}$

————— , ————— , —————
smallest

Draw the time on each clock. Fill in each blank with the correct answer.

14. Mary left her house at 10:30 A.M. 30 minutes later, she reached her school. At what time did Mary reach her school?

30 minutes later

Mary reached her school at ——————.

15. Leo has a guitar lesson every Saturday. His lesson lasts 1 hour. If his guitar lesson ends at 2:30 P.M., at what time does it start?

His guitar lesson starts at _____.

16. All the Grade 1 and 2 students have recess at 9:45 A.M. Recess ends 30 minutes later. At what time does recess end?

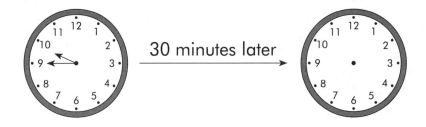

Recess ends at _____.

Do the following story problems. Show your work in the space below.

17. Anton and Jack shared a dish of nachos. If Anton ate $\frac{1}{2}$ of it, how much did Jack eat?

Jack ate _____ of the dish of nachos.

Singapore Math Practice Level 2B

18. Deepak ate $\frac{2}{6}$ of a melon. John ate $\frac{3}{6}$ of the melon. What fraction of the melon did they eat?

They ate _____ of the melon.

19. Harry poured a glass of milk. He drank $\frac{4}{7}$ of it. What fraction of the milk was left in the glass?

_____ of the milk was left in the glass.

20. Tariq borrows a book from the library. He reads $\frac{2}{5}$ of it. What fraction of the book does Tariq need to read in order to complete it?

Tariq needs to read _____ of the book in order to complete it.

Singapore Math Practice Level 2B

Unit 14: VOLUME

Examples:

1.

   Cup A   Cup B   Cup C

   (a) Which cup contains the most water?   **Cup A**

   (b) Which cup contains the least water?   **Cup B**

2.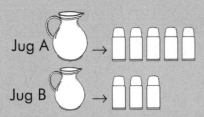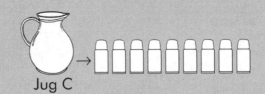

   (a) Which jug contains the least water?   **Jug B**

   (b) Which jug contains the most water?   **Jug C**

   (c) How many fewer flasks of water can Jug A hold than Jug C? $9 - 5 = \underline{4}$

   (d) How many more flasks of water can Jug C hold than Jug B? $9 - 3 = \underline{6}$

3. How many liters of water does the container hold?

   The container holds **3** liters of water.

4. Uncle Norman filled 6 fish tanks with water. Each fish tank contained 4 gallons of water. How many gallons of water did Uncle Norman use to fill the fish tanks?

   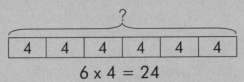

   $6 \times 4 = 24$

   Uncle Norman used **24** gallons of water to fill the fish tanks.

Singapore Math Practice Level 2B

Fill in each blank with *more* or *less*.

1.

(a) Bottle A contains _____ water than Bottle B.

(b) Bottle B contains _____ water than Bottle A.

2.

(a) Cup B contains _____ water than Cup A.

(b) Cup A contains _____ water than Cup B.

Fill in each blank with the correct answer.

3.

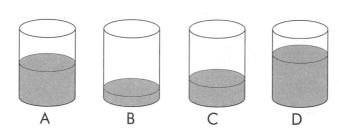

(a) Container _____ has the greatest volume of water.

(b) Container _____ has the least volume of water.

Singapore Math Practice Level 2B

4.

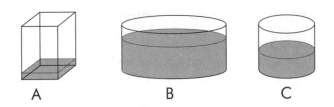

A   B   C

(a)   Container _____ has the greatest volume of water.

(b)   Container _____ has the least volume of water.

5.

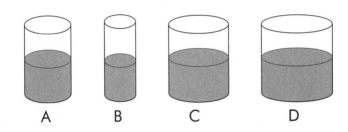

A   B   C   D

(a)   Container _____ has the greatest volume of water.

(b)   Container _____ has the least volume of water.

6.   Study the pictures carefully. Fill in each blank with the correct answer.

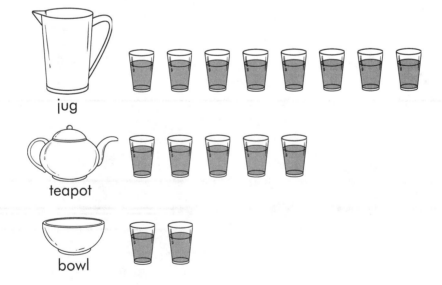

jug

teapot

bowl

(a)   The _____ holds the greatest volume of water.

(b)   The _____ holds the least volume of water.

Singapore Math Practice Level 2B

(c)   The teapot holds _____ more glasses of water than the bowl.

(d)   The bowl holds _____ fewer glasses of water than the jug.

Write the volume of water in each container on the lines below.

7.

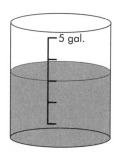

_____ gal. of water

9.

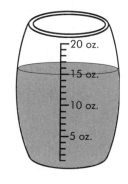

_____ oz. of water

8.

_____ L of water

10.

_____ L of water

Look at each picture carefully. Fill in the blanks with the correct answers.

11.

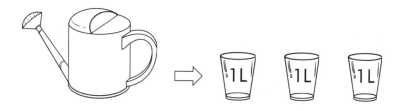

Thomas used _____ L of water to water his plants.

12.

Josefina used _____ gal. of water to wash laundry.

13.

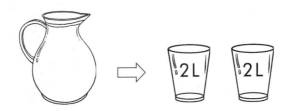

Amy makes _____ L of iced tea.

14.

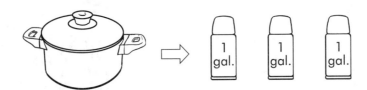

Mother makes _____ gal. of soup.

Solve the following story problems. Show your work in the space below.

15. Lily fills an empty fish tank with 2 buckets of water. Each bucket can hold 2 gal. of water. How many gallons of water are in the fish tank?

There are _____ gal. of water in the fish tank.

Singapore Math Practice Level 2B

16. Mrs. Simon prepares 3 L of iced tea. Mrs. Suzuki prepares 5 L of lemonade. How many liters of drinks do they prepare altogether?

They prepare _____ L of drinks altogether.

17. Darius fills an empty tank with 4 gal. of water. Jack adds 3 gal. of water. Diego adds another 5 gal. of water. How much water can the tank hold?

The tank can hold _____ gal. of water.

18. Ayesha buys 8 L of orange juice. She gives 2 L of juice to Jane. How much orange juice does Ayesha have left?

Ayesha has _____ L of orange juice left.

19. Mr. Benson filled his car with 10 gal. of gas on Monday. He filled his car with 20 gal. of gas on Thursday. How many gallons of gas in all did Mr. Benson put in his car?

Mr. Benson put _____ gal. of gas in his car in all.

20. Maddy fills an empty container with 16 L of water. She then pours all the water equally into some jugs. Each jug holds 4 L of water. How many jugs does she use?

She uses _____ jugs.

Unit 15: GRAPHS

Examples:

The graph below shows the number of students in a class who went on different field trips throughout the year.

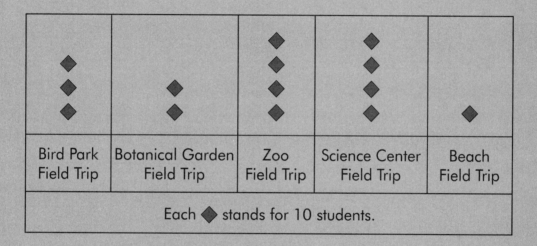

(a)   How many students went on the zoo field trip?   4 x 10 = **40**

(b)   How many students went on the beach field trip?   1 x 10 = **10**

(c)   How many more students went on the zoo field trip than the bird park field trip?

$$4 - 3 = 1$$
$$1 \times 10 = \underline{\mathbf{10}}$$

(d)   How many fewer students went on the beach field trip than the botanical garden field trip?

$$2 - 1 = 1$$
$$1 \times 10 = \underline{\mathbf{10}}$$

(e)   How many students went on all the field trips throughout the year?

$$3 + 2 + 4 + 4 + 1 = 14$$
$$14 \times 10 = \underline{\mathbf{140}}$$

Singapore Math Practice Level 2B

1. Angelo and Michael went to the zoo and saw these animals.
    They drew a picture graph to show the number of each animal.

Animals in the zoo

Monkeys	★ ★ ★ ★ ★ ★
Lions	★ ★
Giraffes	★ ★ ★ ★
Zebras	★ ★ ★
Snakes	★ ★ ★

Each ★ stands for 4 animals.

(a) They saw _____ giraffes.

(b) They saw _____ monkeys.

(c) They saw _____ more giraffes than lions.

(d) They saw _____ fewer snakes than monkeys.

(e) They saw the most _____.

(f) They saw the fewest _____.

Singapore Math Practice Level 2B

2. Study the picture graph carefully. Fill in each blank with the correct answer.

Cartons of milk sold in a week

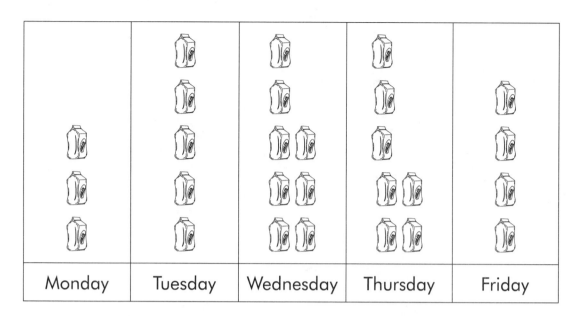

(a) The most cartons of milk were sold on _____.

(b) 50 cartons of milk were sold on Tuesday.

Each 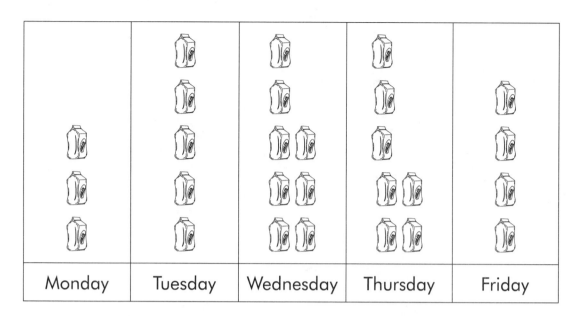 stands for _____ carton(s) of milk.

(c) _____ cartons of milk were sold on Friday.

(d) _____ more cartons of milk were sold on Thursday than on Friday.

(e) _____ fewer cartons of milk were sold on Monday than on Friday.

(f) _____ cartons of milk were sold on Tuesday and Thursday.

Singapore Math Practice Level 2B

3. Below is a chart that shows the animals that Aiden's classmates keep as pets.

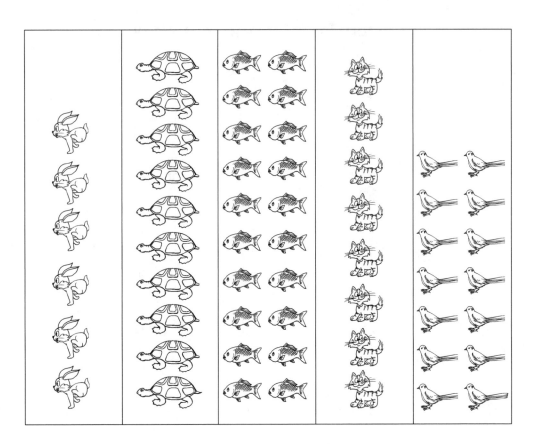

Help Aiden complete the picture graph below.

Rabbits	Turtles	Fish	Cats	Birds

Each ☆ stands for 2 pets.

Singapore Math Practice Level 2B

4. Study the picture graph below. Fill in each blank with the correct answer.

Number of books sold in a bookstore

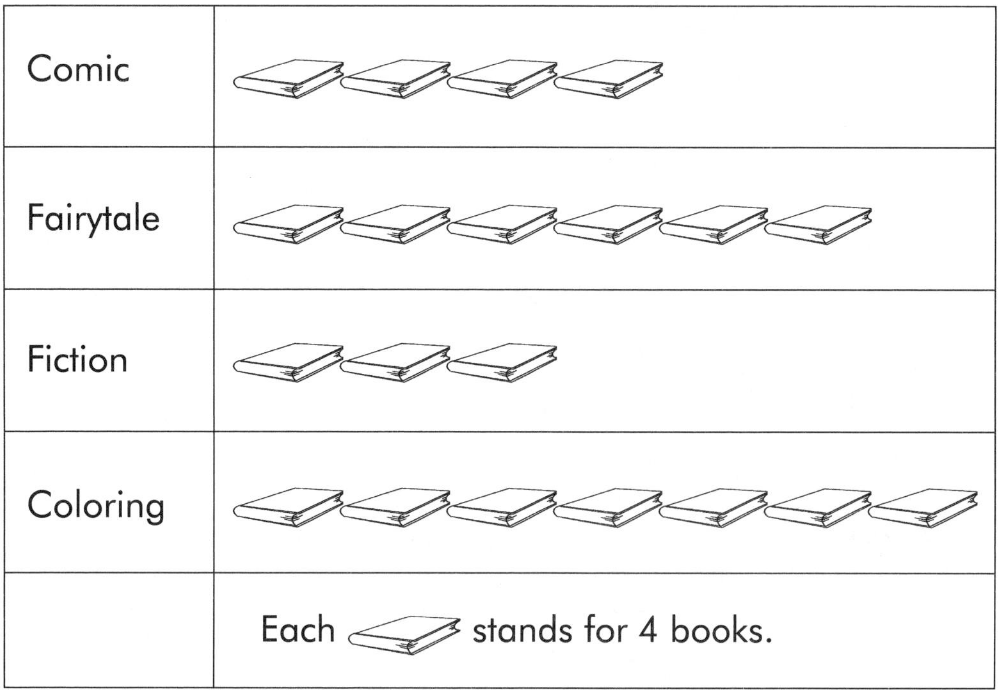

Comic	
Fairytale	
Fiction	
Coloring	
	Each stands for 4 books.

(a) _____ books were the most popular.

(b) _____ books were the least popular.

(c) 4 fewer fairytale books were sold than _____ books.

(d) _____ more comic books were sold than fiction books.

(e) _____ fewer comic books were sold than coloring books.

Singapore Math Practice Level 2B

5. Study the picture graph below. Fill in each blank with the correct answer.

Number of people at the movies

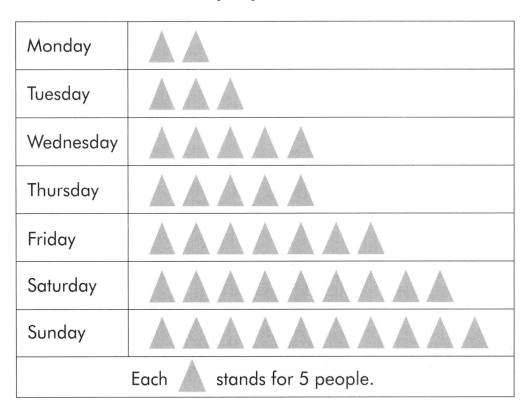

Monday	
Tuesday	
Wednesday	
Thursday	
Friday	
Saturday	
Sunday	

Each ▲ stands for 5 people.

(a) _____ people went to the movies on Wednesday.

(b) _____ more people went to the movies on Friday than on Tuesday.

(c) 2 children went to the movies on Monday. There were _____ adults at the movies on Monday.

(d) _____ people went to the movies over the weekend.

(e) 16 adults went to the movies on Thursday. There were _____ children at the movies on Thursday.

Singapore Math Practice Level 2B

REVIEW 3

Write the volume of water in each container on the lines below.

1.

_____ L of water

2.

_____ gal. of water

3.

_____ L of water

Singapore Math Practice Level 2B

Fill in each blank with the correct answer.

4.   **Favorite dinners of a group of children**

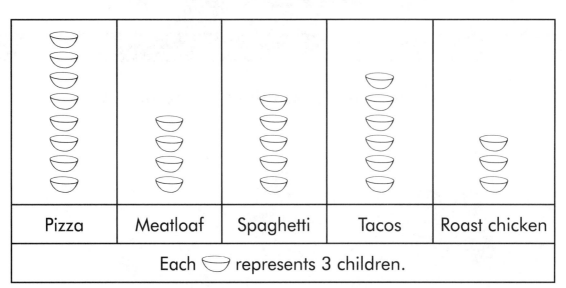

(a)   The number of children who like to eat tacos is _____.

(b)   The number of children who like to eat spaghetti is _____.

(c)   There are _____ fewer children who like to eat roast chicken than tacos.

(d)   There are _____ more children who like to eat pizza than meatloaf.

(e)   The total number of children who like to eat meatloaf and spaghetti

is _____.

Singapore Math Practice Level 2B

5.

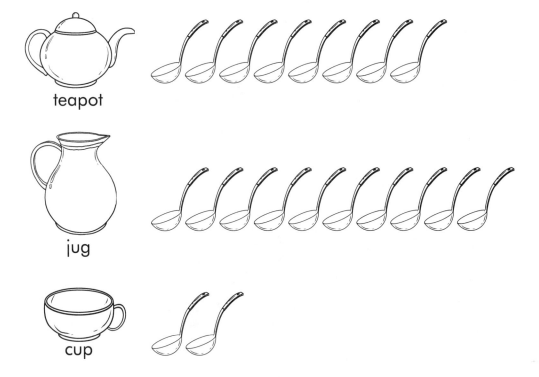

teapot

jug

cup

(a) The container that holds the greatest volume of water is the _____.

(b) The container that holds the least volume of water is the _____.

(c) The jug holds _____ more ladles of water than the cup.

(d) The cup holds _____ fewer ladles of water than the teapot.

(e) The total number of ladles that the 3 containers can hold is _____.

Singapore Math Practice Level 2B

6.   The pictures below show the types of seafood Mr. Kaufman sold at the fish market.

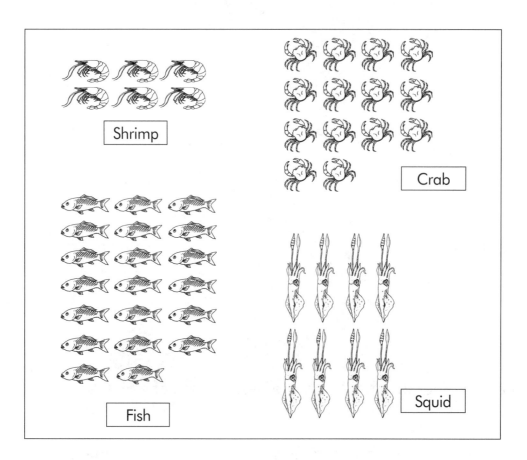

Complete the picture graph.

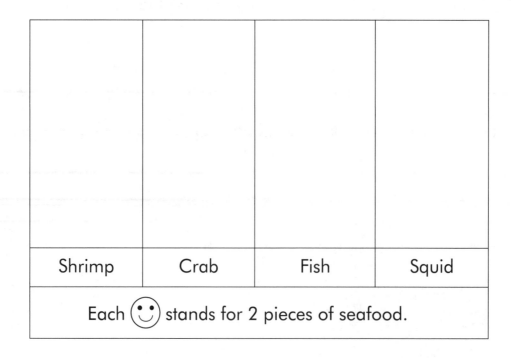

Singapore Math Practice Level 2B

Do the following story problems. Show your work in the space below.

7. Riley bought 2 bottles of fruit juice. Each bottle contained 8 oz. of fruit juice. How many ounces of fruit juice did Riley buy?

Riley bought _____ oz. of fruit juice.

8. Li mixes 10 L of water with 8 L of frozen concentrate to make lemonade.

(a) How many liters of lemonade does Li make?

Li makes _____ L of lemonade.

(b) If Li gives 3 L of lemonade to her neighbor, how many liters of lemonade will she have left?

She will have _____ L of lemonade left.

Singapore Math Practice Level 2B

9. Isabelle collected 10 gal. of rainwater on Monday. She collected 15 gal. of rainwater on Wednesday. How much rainwater did she collect altogether?

She collected _____ gal. of rainwater altogether.

10. Kate bought 5 L of milk over the weekend. She drank 2 L of milk on Monday and Tuesday. How much milk was left?

_____ L of milk was left.

Singapore Math Practice Level 2B

11. Andy needed to buy 20 gal. of drinks for his birthday party. He bought 10 gal. of drinks from Supermarket A and 5 gal. of drinks from Supermarket B.

(a) How many gallons of drinks did Andy buy?

Andy bought _____ gal. of drinks.

(b) How many more gallons did he need to buy?

He needed to buy _____ more gallons of drinks.

12. Eva bought 2 bottles of liquid detergent. Bottle A contained 8 L of liquid detergent. Bottle B contained 25 L of liquid detergent. How much liquid detergent did Eva buy altogether?

Eva bought _____ L of liquid detergent altogether.

Singapore Math Practice Level 2B

13. Kenji removed some water from a tank using a bucket. The bucket could hold 2 gal. of water. He filled the bucket completely with water 6 times. How much water did he remove from the tank?

Kenji removed _____ gal. of water from the tank.

14. Nick poured 24 L of orange juice into 4 containers equally. How much orange juice was there in each container?

There was _____ L of orange juice in each container.

15. Mrs. Anderson recycles water by collecting used water from the washing machine. She collects 5 buckets of used water every week. Each bucket can hold 3 gal. of used water. How much used water does she collect every week?

She collects _____ gal. of used water every week.

Singapore Math Practice Level 2B

16. Jamie drinks 2 L of water daily. How much water does she drink in 10 days?

She drinks _____ L of water in 10 days.

17. Mr. Tomasek brews 17 gal. of coffee and 25 gal. of tea every day. How much coffee and tea does he brew every day?

He brews _____ gal. of coffee and tea every day.

18. Luisa pours 36 gal. of apple juice equally into some containers. Each container can hold 4 gal. of apple juice. How many containers does she need?

She needs _____ containers.

Singapore Math Practice Level 2B

19. Alyssa bought 8 bottles of detergent. Each bottle of detergent was 2 L. How many liters of detergent did Alyssa buy?

Alyssa bought _____ L of detergent.

20. George used 5 gal. of water to wash a car. How many cars did he wash if he used 35 gal. of water?

He washed _____ cars if he used 35 gal. of water.

Singapore Math Practice Level 2B

Unit 16: LINES AND SURFACES

Examples:

1. This picture is formed using straight lines and curves.

    (a) How many straight lines are there?   <u>2</u> straight lines

    (b) How many curves are there?   <u>2</u> curves

2. The object below is made from a tissue box and a toilet paper roll.

    How many flat surfaces does the object have?   <u>5</u> flat surfaces

Fill in each blank with the correct answer.

1.   **2   3   4   5   7   8**

    Which of the above digits have

    (a)   straight lines only?   _____

    (b)   curves only?   _____

    (c)   straight lines and curves?   _____

Singapore Math Practice Level 2B

2.

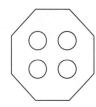

There are _____ straight lines and _____ curves in the above picture.

3.

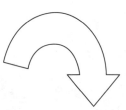

There are _____ straight lines and _____ curves in the above picture.

4.

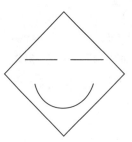

There are _____ straight lines and _____ curve in the above picture.

5.

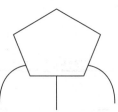

There are _____ straight lines and _____ curves in the above picture.

6.

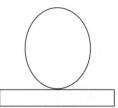

There are _____ straight lines and _____ curve in the above picture.

Singapore Math Practice Level 2B

Look at these objects carefully. Fill in each blank with the correct answer.

7.

The candle has _____ flat surface(s).

8.

The box of tissues has _____ flat surface(s).

9.

The box of ice cream has _____ flat surface(s).

10.

The pot of flowers has _____ flat surface(s).

Singapore Math Practice Level 2B

11.

The container has _____ flat surface(s).

For each object, count the number of flat surfaces. Write the correct answer on the lines below.

12.

_____ flat surfaces

13.

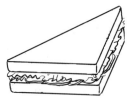

_____ flat surfaces

14.

_____ flat surfaces

15.

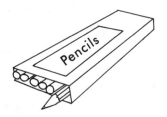

_____ flat surfaces

Unit 17: SHAPES AND PATTERNS

Examples:

1. What shapes are used to form the figure below?

    The shapes are **quarter circle**, **square**, **rectangle**, and **triangle**.

2. Draw a figure using a cone, a cube, and a cylinder.

3. What comes next in the pattern below?

     **?**

     comes next in the pattern.

Singapore Math Practice Level 2B

Identify the shapes below.

1.

_____

2.

_____

3.

_____

4.

_____

5.

_____

6.

_____

7.

_____

Singapore Math Practice Level 2B

Each figure is made of 2 different shapes. Name the 2 shapes.

8.

This figure is made of a

_____ and

a _____.

9.

This figure is made of a

_____ and

a _____.

10.

This figure is made of a

_____ and

a _____.

11.

This figure is made of a

_____ and

a _____.

12.

This figure is made of a

_____ and

a _____.

13. Look at the figure carefully, and fill in each blank with the correct answer.

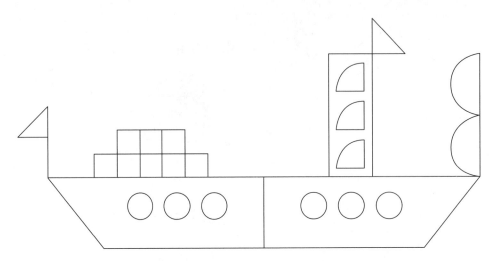

The figure is formed by

(a) _____ rectangles,

(b) _____ triangles,

(c) _____ quarter circles,

(d) _____ circles,

(e) _____ squares, and

(f) _____ semicircles.

Draw lines to show the different shapes that make each figure.

14.

16.

15.

Singapore Math Practice Level 2B

Fill in each blank with the name of the shaded part of each picture.

17.

_____

18.

_____

19.

_____

20.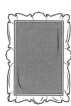

_____

21.

_____

22.

_____

Carefully look at each shape on the left. Draw the same shape on the dot grid on the right.

23.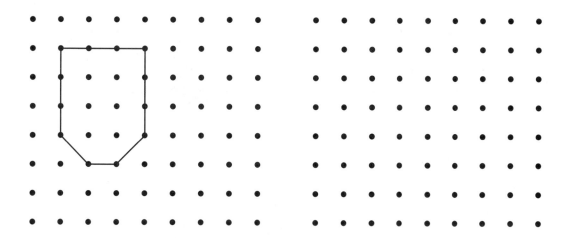

Singapore Math Practice Level 2B

24.

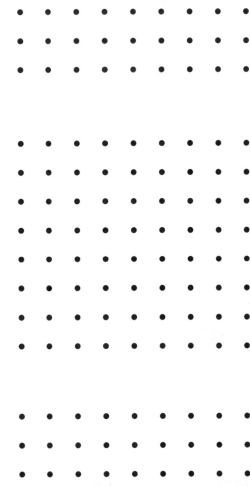

25.

26.

Singapore Math Practice Level 2B

27.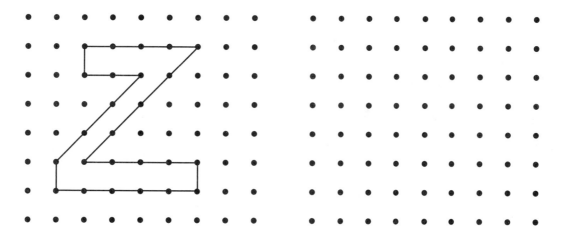

Carefully look at each shape on the left. Draw the same shape on the square grid on the right.

28.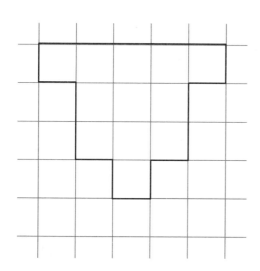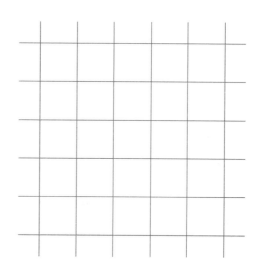

29.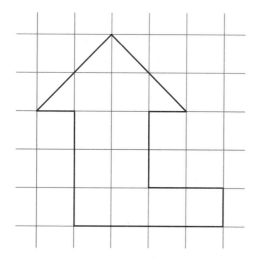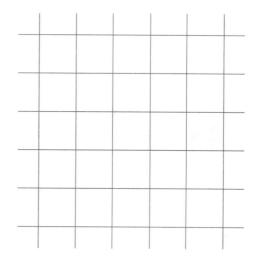

Singapore Math Practice Level 2B

30.

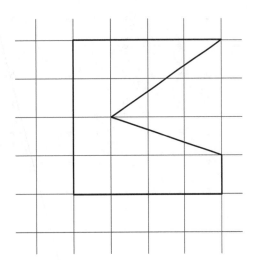

31.

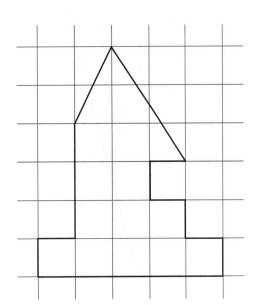
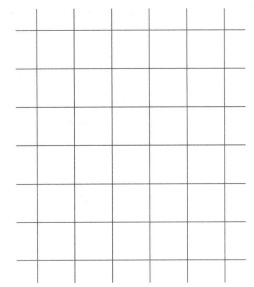

32.

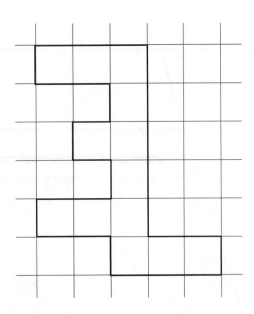

Singapore Math Practice Level 2B

Put a check mark (✓) in the correct box to complete each pattern.

33.

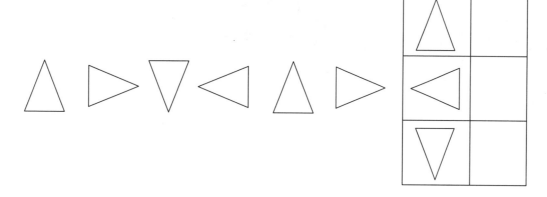

34.

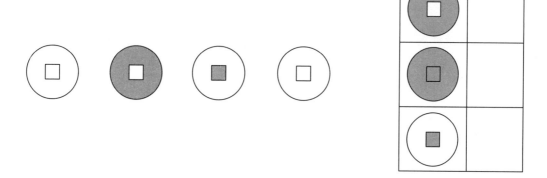

35.

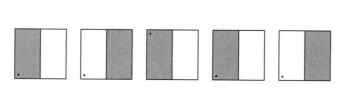
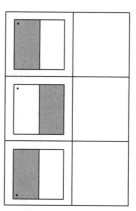

Singapore Math Practice Level 2B

36.

 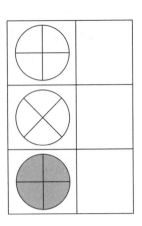

Complete the following patterns.

37.  _____

38. 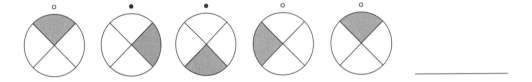 _____

39. 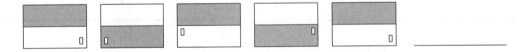 _____

Singapore Math Practice Level 2B

Name the following shapes.

1.

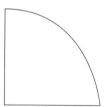

_____

2.

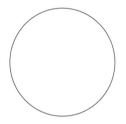

_____

3.

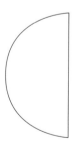

_____

4.

_____

5.

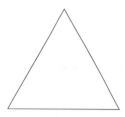

_____

6.

_____

7.

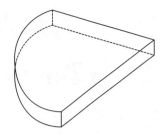

The figure above has _____ flat surface(s).

8.

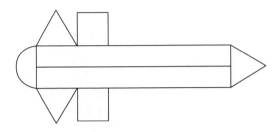

There are _____ triangles, _____ semicircles, _____ rectangles, and _____ squares in the figure above.

Complete the following patterns.

9.

10.

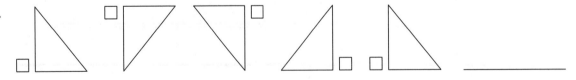

11.

Singapore Math Practice Level 2B

Draw dotted lines on each figure, and identify the shapes that form the figure on the lines below.

12.

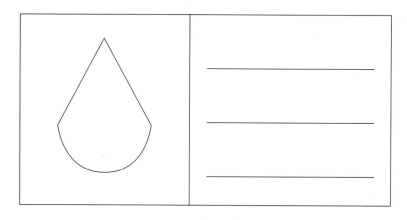

13.

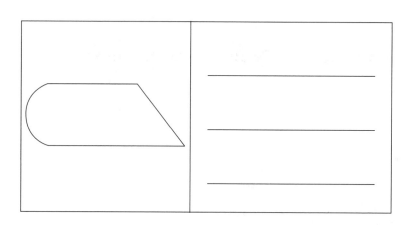

14.

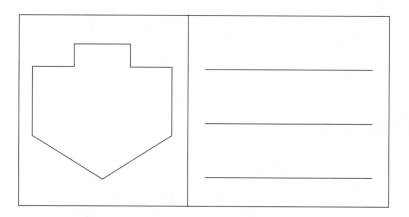

Singapore Math Practice Level 2B

15.

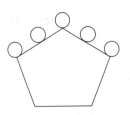

There are _____ straight lines and _____ curves in the above picture.

16.

The battery has _____ flat surface(s).

Look at the shape on the left. Draw the same shape on the square grid on the right.

17.

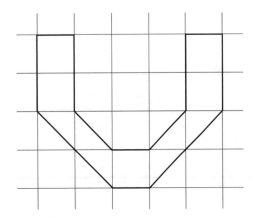 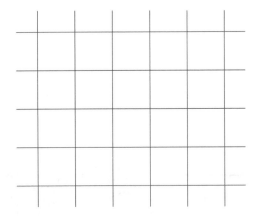

18. Color the objects that have only flat surfaces.

 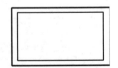  

Singapore Math Practice Level 2B

Carefully look at each shape on the left. Draw the same shape on the dot grid on the right.

19.

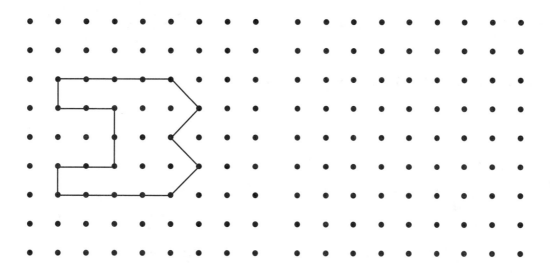

20.

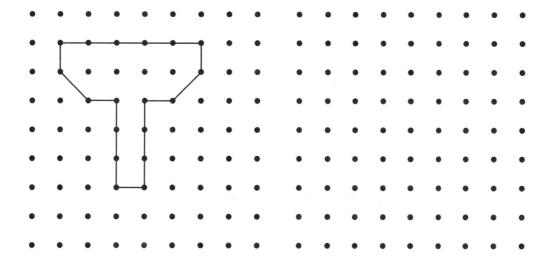

Singapore Math Practice Level 2B

FINAL REVIEW

Fill in each blank with the correct answer.

1. 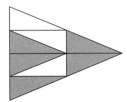 _____ of the figure is shaded.

2. The picture graph below shows the number of eggs Jackson sold in a week.

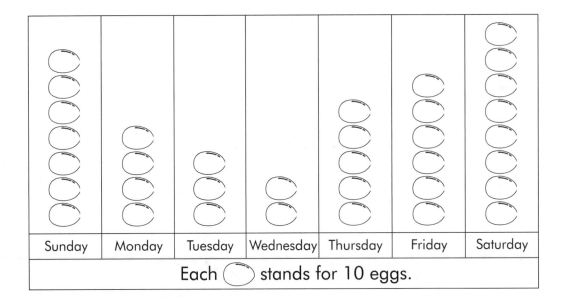

(a) He sold _____ eggs on Thursday.

(b) He sold _____ eggs on Sunday.

(c) He sold _____ more eggs on Friday than on Monday.

(d) He sold _____ fewer eggs on Tuesday than on Saturday.

(e) He sold _____ eggs altogether on Monday and Wednesday.

Singapore Math Practice Level 2B

3. The time shown on the clock is 11:50 A.M.

   30 minutes later, it will be _____.

4. Shade $\frac{1}{4}$ of each figure.

   (a) 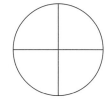   (b)

5.

   Container A can hold _____ L of water.

6. Complete the pattern.

        _____

7. Add 790 and 70 mentally.   _____

8. $\frac{2}{5}$ and _____ make one whole.

9. Draw the minute hand on the clock to show 6:40 P.M.

Singapore Math Practice Level 2B

10. The figure on the right is made of a

    _____ and a _____.

11. Look at the figures carefully.

    A   B   C   D

    Figure _____ does not belong in the group.

12. $\triangle \times \triangle = 100$
    $\bigcirc \times \bigcirc = 25$
    $\triangle \times \bigcirc = $ _____

13. $\frac{1}{10} + \frac{4}{10} + \frac{2}{10} = $ _____

14. The figure below is made of 4 different shapes. Draw dotted lines to show the shapes.

15. Circle the largest fraction.

    $$\frac{1}{12} \quad , \quad \frac{1}{9} \quad , \quad \frac{1}{11}$$

16. $48.30 = _____ dollars and _____ cents

17. Subtract 90 from 345 mentally. _____

18. Express 9,080¢ in dollars. _____

19. Subtract $\frac{2}{11}$ from $\frac{5}{11}$. _____

Singapore Math Practice Level 2B

Solve the following story problems. Show your work in the space below.

20. Alice spent $30 at the supermarket. Sydney spent twice as much as Alice. How much did Sydney spend?

Sydney spent $_____.

21. Patrick gave 5 cans of juice to each of his 7 friends. How many cans of juice did he give to his friends?

He gave _____ cans of juice to his friends.

Singapore Math Practice Level 2B

22. 3 groups of students took part in an art competition. There were 129 students in Group A, 257 students in Group B, and 229 students in Group C. How many students took part in the art competition?

_____ students took part in the art competition.

23. Terrell reads 4 books in a day. How many books will he read in a week?

He will read _____ books in a week.

Singapore Math Practice Level 2B

24. Tyler and Jack make 600 L of fruit punch for an event. If Tyler makes 228 L of fruit punch, how many liters of fruit punch does Jack make?

Jack makes _____ L of fruit punch.

25. Malak received $50 from his aunt and $30 from his uncle on his birthday. How much money did Malak receive in all?

Malak received $_____ in all.

CHALLENGE QUESTIONS

Solve the following problems on another sheet of paper.

1. The chart below shows the number of pieces of clothing Mrs. Robinson sewed.

Number of days	1	3	6
Pieces of clothing	4	12	24

   How many pieces of clothing did Mrs. Robinson sew in 10 days?

2. Sam is 12 years old. His mother is 3 times his age. His father is 5 years older than his mother. How much older is Sam's father than Sam?

3. Use numbers from 10 to 18 to make each vertical and horizontal line equal to the numbers in the shaded boxes. Each number can be used only once.

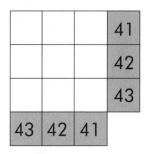

4. Five minutes before recess, Carlos and Henry looked at their watches. Carlos's watch was 5 minutes faster than the classroom clock. Henry's watch was 5 minutes slower than the classroom clock. If Carlos's watch showed 9:50 A.M., what was the time shown on Henry's watch?

5. $\heartsuit + \triangle = 120$

   $\heartsuit + \heartsuit = 80$

   $\heartsuit + \triangle + \triangle + \triangle = $ _____

6. The product of 2 numbers is 50. The result of the division of the 2 numbers is 2. What are the 2 numbers?

Singapore Math Practice Level 2B

7. Christopher had a bottle of orange juice. He gave some juice to his best friend. He then gave half of the remaining juice to his neighbor. He was left with $\frac{1}{4}$ of the bottle of orange juice. What fraction of the bottle of orange juice did Christopher give to his best friend?

8. Austin spent an hour watching cartoons followed by 2 hours of a nap, and 3 hours of homework. If Austin completed his homework at 10 P.M., what time did he start watching cartoons?

9. How many triangles are there in the figure shown below?
   (Hint: The triangles do not need to all be the same size.)

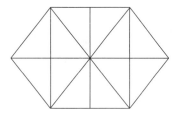

10. Fill in the blank with the correct answer.

   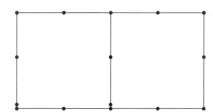

11. Winnie uses some sticks to form 2 squares as shown below. How would you rearrange 4 matchsticks to form 3 rectangles?

12. It took Rico 30 minutes to wash his father's car and an hour to mow the lawn. Then, he took a 20-minute bath. By the time he stepped out of the bathroom, the hour hand pointed to 1 and the minute hand pointed to 4. On the clock, show the time Rico started to wash his father's car.

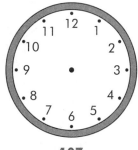

Singapore Math Practice Level 2B

SOLUTIONS
Singapore Math Practice Level 2B

Unit 10: Mental Calculations

1. 64 + 10 = 74
    74 − 2 = **72**
2. 89 + 10 = 99
    99 − 3 = **96**
3. 26 + 10 = 36
    36 − 5 = **31**
4. 18 + 10 = 28
    28 − 1 = **27**
5. 57 + 10 = 67
    67 − 4 = **63**
6. 45 + 10 = 55
    55 − 2 = **53**
7. 37 + 10 = 47
    47 − 5 = **42**
8. 78 + 10 = 88
    88 − 2 = **86**
9. 94 + 10 = 104
    104 − 1 = **103**
10. 56 + 10 = 66
    66 − 3 = **63**
11. 127 + 10 = 137
    137 − 5 = **132**
12. 764 + 10 = 774
    774 − 1 = **773**
13. 2 + 6 = 8
    260 + 8 = **268**
14. 948 + 10 = 958
    958 − 2 = **956**
15. 435 + 10 = 445
    445 − 3 = **442**
16. 4 + 6 = 10
    580 + 10 = **590**
17. 623 + 10 = 633
    633 − 1 = **632**
18. 806 + 10 = 816
    816 − 1 = **815**
19. 366 + 10 = 376
    376 − 5 = **371**
20. 119 + 10 = 129
    129 − 4 = **125**
21. 3 + 6 = 9
    510 + 9 = **519**
22. 30 + 20 = 50
    806 + 50 = **856**
23. 20 + 80 = 100
    703 + 100 = **803**
24. 90 + 70 = 160
    100 + 160 = **260**
25. 20 + 40 = 60
    408 + 60 = **468**

26. 762 + 100 = 862
    862 − 30 = **832**
27. 503 + 100 = 603
    603 − 10 = **593**
28. 869 + 100 = 969
    969 − 20 = **949**
29. 20 + 60 = 80
    603 + 80 = **683**
30. 700 + 200 = 900
    900 + 70 = **970**
31. 300 + 600 = 900
    900 + 23 = **923**
32. 100 + 800 = 900
    900 + 65 = **965**
33. 200 + 500 = 700
    700 + 48 = **748**
34. 600 + 300 = 900
    900 + 57 = **957**
35. 100 + 700 = 800
    800 + 95 = **895**
36. 100 + 200 = 300
    300 + 8 = **308**
37. 500 + 400 = 900
    900 + 88 = **988**
38. 600 + 100 = 700
    700 + 45 = **745**
39. 100 + 600 = 700
    700 + 99 = **799**
40. 700 + 200 = 900
    900 + 56 = **956**
41. 52 − 10 = 42
    42 + 5 = **47**
42. 46 − 10 = 36
    36 + 1 = **37**
43. 81 − 10 = 71
    71 + 2 = **73**
44. 30 − 10 = 20
    20 + 3 = **23**
45. 8 − 3 = 5
    80 + 5 = **85**
46. 9 − 5 = 4
    70 + 4 = **74**
47. 4 − 4 = 0
    60 + 0 = **60**
48. 28 − 10 = 18
    18 + 1 = **19**
49. 3 − 1 = 2
    90 + 2 = **92**
50. 9 − 7 = 2
    50 + 2 = **52**

51. 620 − 10 = 610
    610 + 5 = **615**
52. 404 − 10 = 394
    394 + 4 = **398**
53. 5 − 4 = 1
    870 + 1 = **871**
54. 10 − 2 = 8
    730 + 8 = **738**
55. 9 − 9 = 0
    510 + 0 = **510**
56. 264 − 10 = 254
    254 + 3 = **257**
57. 9 − 6 = 3
    320 + 3 = **323**
58. 183 − 10 = 173
    173 + 5 = **178**
59. 6 − 3 = 3
    910 + 3 = **913**
60. 534 − 10 = 524
    524 + 2 = **526**
61. 415 − 100 = 315
    315 + 70 = **385**
62. 338 − 100 = 238
    238 + 10 = **248**
63. 80 − 60 = 20
    507 + 20 = **527**
64. 60 − 50 = 10
    800 + 10 = **810**
65. 100 − 10 = 90
    509 + 90 = **599**
66. 80 − 20 = 60
    201 + 60 = **261**
67. 50 − 40 = 10
    708 + 10 = **718**
68. 90 − 70 = 20
    405 + 20 = **425**
69. 164 − 100 = 64
    64 + 20 = **84**
70. 626 − 100 = 526
    526 + 40 = **566**
71. 700 − 300 = 400
    400 + 58 = **458**
72. 800 − 600 = 200
    200 + 34 = **234**
73. 900 − 800 = 100
    100 + 5 = **105**
74. 600 − 500 = 100
    100 + 31 = **131**
75. 900 − 900 = 0
    0 + 78 = **78**
76. 500 − 100 = 400
    400 + 5 = **405**
77. 700 − 400 = 300
    300 + 84 = **384**
78. 400 − 200 = 200
    200 + 35 = **235**
79. 800 − 700 = 100
    100 + 76 = **176**
80. 900 − 800 = 100
    100 + 80 = **180**

Unit 11: Money

1. (a) **$10.00**
    (b) **$2.50**
    (c) **$44.40**
    (d) **$39.85**
    (e) **$67.90**
    (f) **$50.05**
    (g) **$19.70**
    (h) **87¢**
    (i) **$12.15**
    (j) **$20.25**
2. (a) twelve, thirty
    (b) forty-five, forty-five
    (c) sixty-seven, five
    (d) fifteen, fifty-five
    (e) seven, ninety
    (f) eleven, eighty
    (g) thirty-six, sixty
    (h) twenty, fifteen
    (i) fifty-nine, ninety-five
    (j) seventy, seventy
3. 10¢ + 10¢ + 5¢ + 5¢ + 5¢ + 5¢ = **40¢**
4. $5 + $1 + $1 + $0.50 = **$7.50**
5. (3 × $10) + (4 × $5) + $0.25 + $0.25 + $0.10 + $0.10 + $0.05 + $0.05 + $0.05 = **$50.85**
6. $10 + $5 + $1 + (4 × $0.25) + $0.10 = **$17.10**
7. (2 × $5) + (4 × $1) + $0.10 + (3 × $0.05) = **$14.25**
8. 50¢ + 10¢ = **60¢**
9. $10.00 + $0.50 = **$10.50**
10. $11.00 + $0.10 = **$11.10**
11. $7.00 + $0.05 = **$7.05**
12. $2.00 + $0.40 = **$2.40**
13. (a) **225**
    (b) **1,050**
    (c) **3,575**
    (d) **5,005**
    (e) **2,735**
    (f) **8,905**
    (g) **10,030**
    (h) **4,040**
    (i) **1,595**
    (j) **2,055**
14. (a) **4.16**
    (b) **18.75**
    (c) **30.05**
    (d) **8.05**
    (e) **17.50**
    (f) **9.60**
    (g) **10.05**
    (h) **76.00**
    (i) **0.18**
    (j) **0.59**
15. (a) **32.50, 26.50**
    (b) **George**
16. (a) **45.90, 55.85**
    (b) **Marcos**
17. (a) **67.80, 65.90**
    (b) **65.90, 67.80**
    (c) **Mrs. Morales**
18. (a) **19.60**
    (b) **26.50**
    (c) **Samira**
    (d) **Kate**

Singapore Math Practice Level 2B

19.

| $3 | $3 | $3 | $3 | $3 | $3 |

6 × $3 = $18
She paid **$18** for the books.

20.

peach | 55¢ |
banana | ? | 25¢ |

55¢ − 25¢ = 30¢
55¢ + 30¢ = 85¢
The total cost of the peach and the banana is **85¢**.

21.

Aunt Rose | $350 |
Uncle James | | $190 | ?

$350 + $190 = $540
Uncle James earns $540 in a week.
$350 + $540 = $890
Both of them earn **$890** in a week.

22.

$100
| $29 | ? |

$100 − $29 = $71
She received **$71** in change.

23.

$40
| ? | ? | ? | ? | ? | ? | ? | ? | ? | ? |

$40 ÷ 10 = $4
He spends **$4** per day.

Review 1

1. **$99.09**
2. 814 + 100 = 914
   914 − 10 = **904**
3. **fifty-five**, **fifteen**
4. $62.00 + $0.55 = **$62.55**
5. **6,285¢**
6. 600 + 200 = 800
   800 + 4 = **804**
7. (a) **35.55, 30.05**
   (b) **Jerome**
8. 546 − 10 = 536
   536 + 1 = **537**
9. **$38.40**
10. 743 − 100 = 643
    643 + 40 = **683**
11. $36.00 + $0.10 = **$36.10**
12. (a) **42, 45**
    (b) **Uncle Sam**
13. **one hundred**, **ten**
14. 686 + 10 = 696
    696 − 5 = **691**
15. 700 − 400 = 300
    300 + 12 = **312**
16.

?
| $2 | $2 | $2 | $2 | $2 | $2 | $2 |

7 × $2 = $14
Emma saves **$14** in a week.

17.

$50
| ? | $2 |

$50 − $2 = $48
The calculator cost **$48**.

18.

| $49 | $35 |
?

$49 + $35 = $84
She spent **$84** in all.

19.

?
| $7 | $7 | $7 |

3 × $7 = $21
Uncle Ronald gives **$21** to his children in all.

20.

$60
| ? | ? | ? | ? | ? | ? |

$60 ÷ 6 = $10
Each towel costs **$10**.

Unit 12: Fractions

1. ✓
2.
3. ✓
4.
5. $\frac{1}{4}$
6. $\frac{3}{8}$
7. $\frac{2}{6}$
8. $\frac{7}{12}$
9. $\frac{4}{7}$

Possible answers:

10.

11.

12.

13.

14.

15. (a) **2**

    (b) **4**

    (c) $\frac{2}{4}$

    (d) $\frac{2}{4}$

16. (a) **4**

    (b) **6**

    (c) $\frac{4}{6}$

    (d) $\frac{2}{6}$

17. (a) **4**, **8**

    (b) $\frac{4}{8}$

18. (a) **2**, **5**

    (b) $\frac{2}{5}$

19. (a) **6**, **7**

    (b) $\frac{6}{7}$

20. (a) **6**

    (b) $\frac{2}{8}$

    (c) $\frac{6}{8}$

    (d) $\frac{2}{8}$, $\frac{6}{8}$

21. (a) **2**

    (b) $\frac{3}{5}$

    (c) $\frac{2}{5}$

    (d) $\frac{3}{5}$, $\frac{2}{5}$

22. $\frac{2}{3}$

23. $\frac{1}{2}$

24. $\frac{4}{7}$

25. $\frac{7}{11}$

26. $\frac{3}{12}$

27. $\frac{3}{5}$

28. $\frac{2}{8}$

29. $\frac{6}{9}$

30. $\frac{3}{4}$

31. $\frac{5}{6}$

32. $\left(\frac{1}{2}\right)$

33. $\left(\frac{3}{6}\right)$

34. $\left(\frac{5}{7}\right)$

35. $\left(\frac{2}{6}\right)$

36. $\left(\frac{1}{5}\right)$

37. $\left(\frac{6}{12}\right)$

38. $\frac{1}{8}$

    $\frac{3}{8}$

    $\left(\frac{5}{8}\right)$

39. $\left(\frac{2}{6}\right)$

    $\frac{2}{8}$

    $\frac{2}{10}$

40. $\frac{1}{4}$

    $\frac{2}{4}$

    $\left(\frac{3}{4}\right)$

41. $\frac{3}{9}$

    $\left(\frac{2}{9}\right)$

42. $\frac{4}{5}$

    $\left(\frac{4}{8}\right)$

43. $\frac{8}{10}$

    $\left(\frac{6}{10}\right)$

44. $\left(\frac{1}{5}\right)$

45. $\left(\frac{2}{8}\right)$

46. $\left(\frac{3}{8}\right)$

47. $\left(\frac{2}{3}\right)$

48. $\left(\frac{4}{5}\right)$

49. $\left(\frac{7}{10}\right)$

50. $\left(\frac{5}{5}\right)$

51. $\left(\frac{1}{10}\right)$

Singapore Math Practice Level 2B

52. $\left(\dfrac{5}{7}\right)$

53. $\left(\dfrac{1}{5}\right)$

54. $\left(\dfrac{4}{7}\right)$

55. $\left(\dfrac{3}{9}\right)$

56. $\dfrac{5}{6}, \dfrac{3}{6}, \dfrac{1}{6}$

57. $\dfrac{2}{3}, \dfrac{2}{8}, \dfrac{2}{9}$

58. $\dfrac{4}{10}, \dfrac{4}{11}, \dfrac{4}{12}$

59. $\dfrac{1}{12}, \dfrac{1}{11}, \dfrac{1}{10}$

60. $\dfrac{3}{9}, \dfrac{3}{6}, \dfrac{3}{5}$

61. $\dfrac{5}{12}, \dfrac{5}{10}, \dfrac{5}{9}$

62. $\dfrac{3}{8}$

63. $\dfrac{7}{10}$

64. $\dfrac{10}{12}$

65. $\dfrac{6}{7}$

66. $\dfrac{8}{9}$

67. $\dfrac{4}{5}$

68. $\dfrac{4}{6}$

69. $\dfrac{6}{11}$

70. $\dfrac{2}{4}$

71. $\dfrac{2}{9}$

72. $\dfrac{5}{7}$

73. $\dfrac{9}{10}$

74. $\dfrac{2}{6}$

75. $\dfrac{3}{11}$

76. $\dfrac{3}{8}$

77. $\dfrac{3}{12}$

78.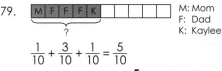

$\dfrac{5}{5} - \dfrac{2}{5} = \dfrac{3}{5}$

$\dfrac{3}{5}$ of the bread is left.

79.
M F F F K   M: Mom
?   F: Dad
             K: Kaylee

$\dfrac{1}{10} + \dfrac{3}{10} + \dfrac{1}{10} = \dfrac{5}{10}$

They have eaten $\dfrac{5}{10}$ of the pizza.

80.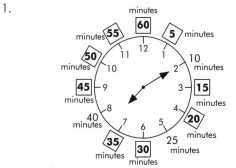

P D D D   P: Pencil case
?   D: Drawing materials

$\dfrac{1}{7} + \dfrac{3}{7} = \dfrac{4}{7}$

She used $\dfrac{4}{7}$ of her weekly allowance.

81.
D D D   D: Drank
?

$\dfrac{8}{8} - \dfrac{3}{8} = \dfrac{5}{8}$

$\dfrac{5}{8}$ of the pitcher of orange juice was left.

82.
C W W W   C: Children
?   W: Women

$\dfrac{1}{6} + \dfrac{3}{6} = \dfrac{4}{6}$

$\dfrac{4}{6}$ of the people at the party are children and women.

Unit 13: Time

1.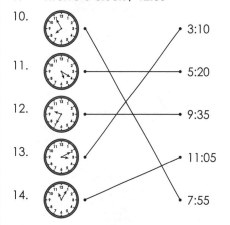

   7:10

2. 4 × 5 minutes = **20**

3. 9 × 5 minutes = **45**

4. 1 × 5 minutes = **5**

5. 3 × 5 minutes = **15**

6. **ten o'clock / 10:00**

7. **five-fifteen / 5:15**

8. **one-thirty / 1:30**

9. **twelve o'clock / 12:00**

10.

11.

12.

13.

14.

3:10
5:20
9:35
11:05
7:55

Singapore Math Practice Level 2B

15.
16.
17.
18.
19.
20.
21.
22.
23.
24.
25.
26.
27.
28.
29.
30.

31. **A.M.**
32. **P.M.**
33. **P.M.**
34. **A.M.**
35. **P.M.**
36. **8:30,**
    8 o'clock / 8:00
37. **5 o'clock / 5:00,**
    4:30
38. **7:30, 6:30**
39. **9 o'clock / 9:00,**
    12 o'clock / 12:00
40. **6:15, 10:15**
41. **11:00 A.M.**

42. **7:00 P.M.**

43. **5:00 A.M.**

44. **4:00 P.M.**

45. **12:00 noon**

Review 2

1. (b)

(c)

2.

3.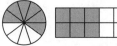

4. **10:25**
5. **5:00 / 5 o'clock**
6. **8:55**
7. **7:30**
8.
9.
10.
11.
12. $\frac{6}{7}, \frac{5}{7}, \frac{1}{7}$
13. $\frac{4}{8}, \frac{5}{8}, \frac{7}{8}$
14.

   11 A.M.
15.

   1:30 P.M.
16.

   10:15 A.M.
17.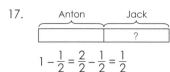

   $1 - \frac{1}{2} = \frac{2}{2} - \frac{1}{2} = \frac{1}{2}$

   Jack ate $\frac{1}{2}$ of the dish of nachos.
18. 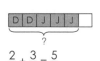   D: Deepak
   J: John

   $\frac{2}{6} + \frac{3}{6} = \frac{5}{6}$

   They ate $\frac{5}{6}$ of the melon.
19. 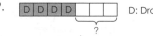   D: Drank

---

$1 - \frac{4}{7} = \frac{7}{7} - \frac{4}{7} = \frac{3}{7}$

$\frac{3}{7}$ of the milk was left in the glass.

20. 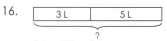   R: Read

   $1 - \frac{2}{5} = \frac{5}{5} - \frac{2}{5} = \frac{3}{5}$

   Tariq needs to read $\frac{3}{5}$ of the book in order to complete it.

Unit 14: Volume

1. (a) **more**
   (b) **less**
2. (a) **less**
   (b) **more**
3. (a) **D**
   (b) **B**
4. (a) **B**
   (b) **A**
5. (a) **D**
   (b) **B**
6. (a) **jug**
   (b) **bowl**
   (c) $5 - 2 = $ **3**
   (d) $8 - 2 = $ **6**
7. **3**
8. **5**
9. **15**
10. **2**
11. $1 + 1 + 1 = $ **3**
12. $2 + 2 + 2 + 2 = $ **8**
13. $2 + 2 = $ **4**
14. $1 + 1 + 1 = $ **3**
15. | 2 gal. | 2 gal. |
    |---|---|

    2×2 gal. $= 4$ gal.
    The fish tank is filled with **4 gal.** of water.
16. | 3 L | 5 L |
    |---|---|

    $3 L + 5 L = 8 L$
    They prepare **8 L** of drink altogether.
17. | 4 gal. | 3 gal. | 5 gal. |
    |---|---|---|

    4 gal. + 3 gal. + 5 gal. = 12 gal.
    The tank can hold **12 gal.** of water.
18. | 2 L | ? |
    |---|---|

    8 L

    $8 L - 2 L = 6 L$
    Ayesha has **6 L** of orange juice left.
19. | 10 gal. | 20 gal. |
    |---|---|

    10 gal. + 20 gal. = 30 gal.
    Mr. Benson put **30 gal.** of gas in his car in all.

Singapore Math Practice Level 2B

20.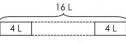

$16\ L \div 4\ L = 4$

She used **4** jugs.

Unit 15: Graphs

1. (a) $4 \times 4 =$ **16**
   (b) $6 \times 4 =$ **24**
   (c) $2 \times 4 = 8$
   $16 - 8 =$ **8**
   (d) $3 \times 4 = 12$
   $24 - 12 =$ **12**
   (e) **monkeys**
   (f) **lions**

2. (a) **Wednesday**
   (b) $50 \div 5 =$ **10**
   (c) $4 \times 10 =$ **40**
   (d) $7 \times 10 = 70$
   $70 - 40 =$ **30**
   (e) $3 \times 10 = 30$
   $40 - 30 =$ **10**
   (f) $50 + 70 =$ **120**

3. Rabbits $\rightarrow 6 \div 2 = 3$☆
   Turtles $\rightarrow 10 \div 2 = 5$☆
   Fish $\rightarrow 20 \div 2 = 10$☆
   Cats $\rightarrow 8 \div 2 = 4$☆
   Birds $\rightarrow 14 \div 2 = 7$☆

	☆☆☆	☆☆		☆☆
☆☆☆	☆☆☆☆☆☆	☆☆☆☆☆	☆☆☆☆	☆☆☆☆ ☆☆
Rabbits	Turtles	Fish	Cats	Birds
Each ☆ stands for 2 pets.				

4. (a) **Coloring**
   $7 \times 4 = 28$
   (b) **Fiction**
   $3 \times 4 = 12$
   (c) **Coloring**
   $6 \times 4 = 24$
   $28 - 24 = 4$
   (d) **4**
   $4 \times 4 = 16$
   $16 - 12 = 4$
   (e) **12**
   $28 - 16 = 12$

5. (a) **25**
   $5 \times 5 = 25$
   (b) **20**
   Friday $\rightarrow 7 \times 5 = 35$
   Tuesday $\rightarrow 3 \times 5 = 15$
   $35 - 15 = 20$
   (c) **8**
   $2 \times 5 = 10$
   $10 - 2 = 8$

(d) **95**
   Saturday $\rightarrow 9 \times 5 = 45$
   Sunday $\rightarrow 10 \times 5 = 50$
   $45 + 50 = 95$
(e) **9**
   $5 \times 5 = 25$
   $25 - 16 = 9$

Review 3

1. **5**
2. **2**
3. **10**
4. (a) $6 \times 3 =$ **18**
   (b) $5 \times 3 =$ **15**
   (c) Roast chicken $\rightarrow 3 \times 3 = 9$
   Tacos $\rightarrow 6 \times 3 = 18$
   $18 - 9 =$ **9**
   (d) Pizza $\rightarrow 8 \times 3 = 24$
   Meatloaf $\rightarrow 4 \times 3 = 12$
   $24 - 12 =$ **12**
   (e) Spaghetti $\rightarrow 5 \times 3 = 15$
   $12 + 15 =$ **27**

5. (a) **jug**
   (b) **cup**
   (c) $10 - 2 =$ **8**
   (d) $8 - 2 =$ **6**
   (e) $8 + 10 + 2 =$ **20**

6. Shrimp $\rightarrow 6 \div 2 = 3$ ☺
   Crab $\rightarrow 14 \div 2 = 7$ ☺
   Fish $\rightarrow 20 \div 2 = 10$ ☺
   Squid $\rightarrow 8 \div 2 = 4$ ☺

	☺☺☺	☺☺ ☺☺	
☺☺☺☺	☺☺	☺☺ ☺☺ ☺☺	☺☺☺☺
Shrimp	Crab	Fish	Squid
Each ☺ stands for 2 pieces of seafood.			

7. [8 oz. | 8 oz.] ?

$2 \times 8\ oz. = 16\ oz.$

Riley bought **16 oz.** of fruit juice.

8. (a) [10 L | 8 L] ?

$10\ L + 8\ L = 18\ L$

Li makes **18 L** of lemonade.

(b) [? | 3 L] 18 L

$18\ L - 3\ L = 15\ L$

She will have **15 L** of lemonade left.

9. [10 gal. | 15 gal.] ?

$10\ gal. + 15\ gal. = 25\ gal.$

She collected **25 gal.** of rainwater altogether.

Singapore Math Practice Level 2B

10.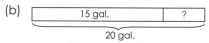

$5 L - 2 L = 3 L$

3 L of milk was left.

11. (a)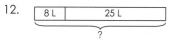

10 gal. + 5 gal. = 15 gal.
Andy bought **15 gal.** of drinks.

(b)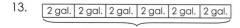

20 gal. – 15 gal. = 5 gal.
He needed to buy **5** more gallons of drinks.

12.

25 L + 8 L = 33 L
Eva bought **33 L** of liquid detergent altogether.

13.

6 × 2 gal. = 12 gal.
He removed **12 gal.** of water from the tank.

14.

24 L ÷ 4 = 6 L
There was **6 L** of orange juice in each container.

15.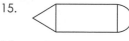

5 × 3 gal. = 15 gal.
She collects **15 gal.** of used water every week.

16.

10 × 2 L = 20 L
She drinks **20 L** of water in 10 days.

17.

17 gal. + 25 gal. = 42 gal.
He brews **42 gal.** of coffee and tea every day.

18.

36 gal. ÷ 4 gal. = 9
She needs **9** containers.

19.

8 × 2 L = 16 L
Alyssa bought **16 L** of detergent.

20.

35 gal. ÷ 5 gal. = 7
He washed **7** cars if he used 35 gal. of water.

Unit 16: Lines and Surfaces

1. (a) **4, 7**
   (b) **3, 8**
   (c) **2, 5**
2. **8, 4**
3. **5, 2**
4. **6, 1**
5. **6, 2**
6. **4, 1**
7. **1**
8. **6**
9. **6**
10. **1**
11. **2**
12. **6**
13. **5**
14. **0**
15. **5**

Unit 17: Shapes and Patterns

1. rectangle
2. triangle
3. square
4. quarter circle
5. circle
6. triangle
7. semicircle
8. triangle, semicircle
9. triangle, rectangle
10. circle, square
11. triangle, quarter circle
12. rectangle, circle
13. (a) **3**
    (b) **4**
    (c) **3**
    (d) **6**
    (e) **8**
    (f) **2**
14.
15.
16.
17. triangle
18. circle
19. semicircle
20. rectangle
21. quarter circle
22. square

Singapore Math Practice Level 2B

23.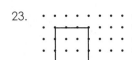

24.

25.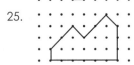

26.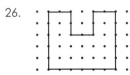

27.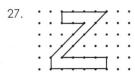

28.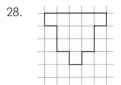

29.

30.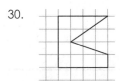

31.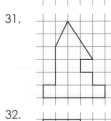

32.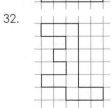

33.

34.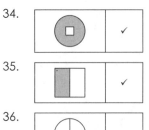

35.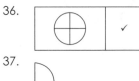

36.

37.

38.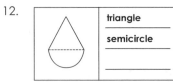

39.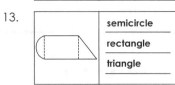

Review 4

1. **circle**
2. **quarter circle**
3. **semicircle**
4. **rectangle**
5. **triangle**
6. **square**
7. **4**
8. **3**, **1**, **2**, **2**
9. △ (the smaller triangle)
10.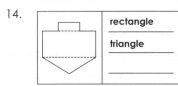
11.

12.

	triangle
	semicircle

13.

	semicircle
	rectangle
	triangle

14.

	rectangle
	triangle

15. **5, 5**
16. **1**
17.

Singapore Math Practice Level 2B

18. Color the **book**, **rectangle**, and **stamp**.

19.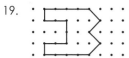

20.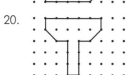

Final Review

1. $\frac{5}{8}$

2. (a) $5 \times 10 = \mathbf{50}$
   (b) $7 \times 10 = \mathbf{70}$
   (c) Monday $\rightarrow 4 \times 10 = 40$
   Friday $\rightarrow 6 \times 10 = 60$
   $60 - 40 = \mathbf{20}$
   (d) Tuesday $\rightarrow 3 \times 10 = 30$
   Saturday $\rightarrow 8 \times 10 = 80$
   $80 - 30 = \mathbf{50}$
   (e) Wednesday $\rightarrow 2 \times 10 = 20$
   $40 + 20 = \mathbf{60}$

3. **12:20 P.M.**

4. (a)

   (b)

5. $1\,L + 1\,L = 2\,L$
   1 jug can hold 2 L of water.
   $3 \times 2\,L = \mathbf{6\,L}$

6.

7. $790 + 100 = 890$
   $890 - 30 = \mathbf{860}$

8. $\frac{5}{5} - \frac{2}{5} = \frac{\mathbf{3}}{\mathbf{5}}$

9.

10. **semicircle, rectangle**

11. **C**
    $\frac{2}{4}$ of Figure C is shaded, while $\frac{1}{4}$ of the rest of the figures are shaded.

12. $10 \times 10 = 100$
    $\triangle = 10$
    $5 \times 5 = 25$
    $\bigcirc = 5$
    $10 \times 5 = \mathbf{50}$

13. $\frac{7}{10}$

14.

15.
    $\frac{1}{9}$ is the largest, and $\frac{1}{12}$ is the smallest.

16. **forty-eight, thirty**

17. $345 - 100 = 245$
    $245 + 10 = \mathbf{255}$

18. **$90.80**

19. $\frac{5}{11} - \frac{2}{11} = \frac{\mathbf{3}}{\mathbf{11}}$

20. Sydney | $30 | $30 | ?
    $30 + $30 = $60
    Sydney spent **$60**.

21. | 5 | 5 | 5 | 5 | 5 | 5 | 5 | ?
    $7 \times 5 = 35$
    He gave **35** cans of juice to his friends.

22. | 129 | 257 | 229 | ?
    $129 + 257 = 386$
    $386 + 229 = 615$
    615 students took part in the art competition.

23. | 4 | 4 | 4 | 4 | 4 | 4 | 4 | ?
    $7 \times 4 = 28$
    He will read **28** books in a week.

24.
    $600\,L - 228\,L = 372\,L$
    Jack makes **372 L** of fruit punch.

25. | $30 | $50 | ?
    $50 + $30 = $80
    Malak received **$80** in all.

Challenge Questions

1. 1 day $\rightarrow$ 4 pieces of clothing
   10 days $\rightarrow 10 \times 4 = 40$ pieces of clothing
   Mrs. Robinson sewed **40** pieces of clothing in 10 days.

2.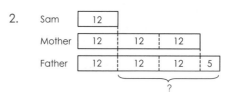

$2 \times 12 = 24$
$24 + 5 = 29$
Sam's father is **29** years older than Sam.

3.

18	10	13	41
11	15	16	42
14	17	12	43
43	42	41	

4.

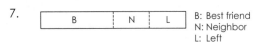

$5 + 5 = 10$
10 min. before 9:50 A.M. is 9:40 A.M.
The time shown on Henry's watch was **9:40 A.M.**

5. $2\heartsuit \rightarrow 80$
$1\heartsuit \rightarrow 80 \div 2 = 40$
$40 + \triangle = 120$
$\triangle = 120 - 40 = 80$
$\heartsuit + \triangle + \triangle + \triangle \rightarrow 40 + 80 + 80 + 80 =$ **280**

6. Use the guess-and-check method.

	1st number	2nd number	1st number × 2nd number
Guess 1	1	50	
Guess 2	2	25	50
Guess 3	5	10	

The result of the division of the 2 numbers in Guess 1 and Guess 2 do not equal 2.
$10 \div 5 = 2$
The 2 numbers are **5** and **10**.

7.

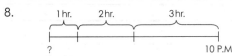

B: Best friend
N: Neighbor
L: Left

Since $\frac{1}{4}$ of the bottle of orange juice was left, the amount of juice Christopher gave to his neighbor was also $\frac{1}{4}$.

$1 - \frac{1}{4} - \frac{1}{4} = \frac{4}{4} - \frac{1}{4} - \frac{1}{4} = \frac{2}{4} = \frac{1}{2}$

Christopher gave his best friend $\frac{2}{4}$ or $\frac{1}{2}$ of the bottle of orange juice.

8.

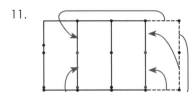

$1 + 2 + 3 = 6$ hr.
6 hr. before 10 P.M. is 4 P.M.
He started watching cartoons at **4 P.M.**

9. **26**
The types of triangles in the figure are ◣, ◢, ▽, △, ◁, ▷, ◳ and ◰.

10. Use the guess-and-check method.
$8 \times 4 = 32$
$8 \div 4 = 2$
$8 + 4 = 12$
$\mathbb{C} - \diamondsuit = 8 - 4 =$ **4**

11.

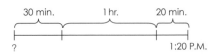

12. Rico stepped out of the bathroom at 1:20 P.M.

30 min. + 1 hr. + 20 min. = 1 hr. 50 min.
1 hr. 50 min. before 1:20 P.M. is 11:30 A.M.

Singapore Math Practice Level 2B

Notes

Notes

Notes

Notes

Notes

Notes

Notes

Notes